J. M. Synge
Interviews and Recollections

Also by E. H. Mikhail

The Social and Cultural Setting of the 1890s
John Galsworthy the Dramatist
Comedy and Tragedy
Sean O'Casey: A Bibliography of Criticism
A Bibliography of Modern Irish Drama 1899–1970
Dissertations on Anglo-Irish Drama:
A Bibliography of Studies 1870–1970
The Sting and the Twinkle: Conversations with Sean O'Casey
(co-editor with John O'Riordan)
J. M. Synge: A Bibliography of Criticism
W. B. Yeats: Interviews and Recollections (2 volumes)
British Drama 1900–1950
Contemporary British Drama 1950–1976

J. M. SYNGE

Interviews and Recollections

Edited by
E. H. Mikhail

Foreword by
Robin Skelton

BOOKS
10 East 53d St., New York 10022
(a division of Harper & Row Publishers, Inc.)

Selection and editorial matter: © E. H. Mikhail 1977

All rights reserved. No part of this publication may be reproduced or transmitted, in any form or by any means, without permission

First published 1977 by
THE MACMILLAN PRESS LTD
London and Basingstoke

Published in the U.S.A. 1977 by
HARPER & ROW PUBLISHERS, INC.
BARNES & NOBLE IMPORT DIVISION

Printed in Great Britain

Library of Congress Cataloging in Publication Data
Main entry under title:

J. M. Synge : interviews and recollections.

Includes index.
 1. Synge, John Millington, 1871–1909—Biography—Addresses, essays, lectures. 2. Dramatists, Irish—19th century—Biography—Addresses, essays, lectures.
 1. Mikhail, E. H.
PR5533.J18   1977   822'.9'12 [B]   75-43223
ISBN 0-06-494817-X

To my wife

Contents

Foreword by Robin Skelton — ix

Preface — xi

Acknowledgements — xiii

INTERVIEWS AND RECOLLECTIONS

A Memory of Synge *W. B. Yeats*	1
John Synge as I knew Him *C. H. H[oughton]*	3
Synge and MacKenna *E. R. Dodds*	7
In the Temple of Fame *Arthur Lynch*	10
Synge *Arthur Lynch*	12
Synge *Stephen MacKenna*	14
First Meeting with Synge *W. B. Yeats*	15
John M. Synge: A Personal Appreciation *D. J. O'Donoghue*	17
An Excitable Man *James Joyce*	20
An 'Un-Irish' Play *Maire Nic Shiubhlaigh*	22
In the Shadow of the Glen *William G. Fay*	26
The Well of the Saints *William G. Fay*	30
With Synge in Connemara *Jack B. Yeats*	32
Synge Watching His Rehearsals *Oliver St John Gogarty*	35
Abbey Theatre Scene	36
I Don't Care a Rap *J. M. Synge*	37
The Author Interviewed	42
Mr. Synge Beaming	42
An Exciting Experience *Walter Starkie*	45
The Playboy of the Western World *William G. Fay*	48
J. M. Synge and the Ireland of his Time *W. B. Yeats*	55
My Memories of John Synge *Pádraic Colum*	62
Synge in Hospital *Joseph Holloway*	70

Synge and the Early Days of the Abbey *Sean O' Mahony Rahilly*	71
The Death of Synge *W. B. Yeats*	74
John M. Synge *John Masefield*	78
Synge *Lady Gregory*	86
Synge *George Moore*	95
Synge and the Irish *John B. Yeats*	106
I Remember J. M. Synge *James Stephens*	107
J. M. Synge *W. R. Rodgers (editor)*	111
Memories of John Synge *Walter Starkie*	131
Index	135

Foreword

The personality of J. M. Synge has always aroused intense curiosity. His contemporaries were clearly baffled by the way in which this product of a highly respectable, extremely conservative, evangelical protestant bourgeois family created drama of such energy and passion. Even his early works seem to owe little to other Irish Nationalist writers. Unlike his contemporaries Yeats, Lady Gregory and A. E., he cut no figure in society. He was the silent observer at literary gatherings. He responded only rarely to the attacks made upon him. He seemed indeed to be a very private man and therefore a mystery.

Any attempt to understand the character of J. M. Synge must take on something of the quality of a detective story. The clues must be gathered together and placed in order before one can hope to see any glimmering of a solution. Perhaps the most important clues are to be found in Synge's own writings and especially in his letters, and in his prose writings. There is however much other evidence which has, until now, been scattered throughout many different books and journals. This is made up of the comments and recollections of Synge's contemporaries and Professor Mikhail has performed a valuable service in bringing all this material together in one volume.

The picture that emerges is perhaps shadowy; the witnesses are sometimes prejudiced and sometimes unreliable. Several of them seem rather to make use of Synge as a character in their own mythologies than to present him objectively. Almost all find that certainty eludes them. It is perhaps the elusiveness of Synge which emerges most clearly from this book. He was of all the Irish writers of his generation the least predictable. It sometimes appears as if, like the poet as described by Keats, he had 'no identity'. In exploring the character of Synge we are indeed exploring a crucial aspect central to the nature of the creative process and also observing, not for the first time, that the man of genius always remains both to his contemporaries and his successors something of an enigma.

ROBIN SKELTON

Preface

It seems ironical to attempt a book on the conversations and recollections of J. M. Synge, the man who lived practically as a recluse. As a lad, he was strangely reserved and even unboyish to a certain extent: he shunned rather than desired companionship; he would hardly take part in the games of his age, and much preferred open-air exercise and solitary rambles in his beloved Dublin mountains to indoor life. In later years, he went a-wandering in strange places, ever and always a sad and lonely man. It was by solitude that he asserted his personality in the gentle, unromantic manner that always was his; and from the very start he was and remained himself and nothing but himself. He seldom told his family or friends about his experiences abroad. 'He had wandered a lot about Europe,' said John Masefield, 'He was silent about all that. I never heard him mention his early life.' During *The Playboy* riots, Synge wrote to one of his correspondents: 'Whether or not I agree with your final interpretation of the whole play is my secret. I follow Goethe's rule, to tell no one what one means in one's writings. I am sure that you will agree that the rule is a good one.'

Nor did Synge mix in intellectual circles. In a social gathering he generally remained an inscrutable listener until drawn out of his shell of reserve. Casual acquaintances found him dull; others thought that he led an intense inward life. James Stephens remembers him as 'somewhat negative to ordinary human beings'. He certainly had no conversation in Bernard Shaw's or George Moore's sense of the word. John B. Yeats described his conversation as 'rare and sudden'. According to Oliver St John Gogarty, 'The rush-bottomed chair next to him was filled by talker after talker, but Synge was not talking. He was answering.' Arthur Lynch recalls, 'When I knew him he suffered rather from undue diffidence. . . . It was difficult to get him to speak at all.' 'In a room he was a listener;' reminisces Pádraic Colum, 'he kept neither aloof nor apart, but in a city of people who talked eagerly, he, with that strongly modelled head of his so well up and with his air as of a foreign student, was noticeably quiet and unassuming.' W. B. Yeats said that he 'cannot imagine him anxious to impress or convince in any company, or saying more than was sufficient to keep the talk circling'. Synge's constant effort thus seemed to be to make others forget that he was there, so that he might observe them without their knowing it. All that he cared for was concrete experience. A man of few

opinions, with no bent for philosophic generalisations, he was content to watch life from an exclusively artistic standpoint.

The testimony of Synge's friends about his brooding silence and impersonality makes one realise, however, that they saw only one side of him. It is hoped that the present collection of conversations and recollections will throw further light on this shy-mannered man, whose literary fame and world-wide success as a playwright never spoiled his unaffected simplicity.

University of Lethbridge E. H. MIKHAIL
Alberta, Canada

Acknowledgements

I am grateful to Professor A. Norman Jeffares for his perceptive criticism of the manuscript of this book.

It is also a pleasant duty to record my appreciation to the staff of the University of Lethbridge Library; the British Library, London; the National Library of Ireland, Dublin; Trinity College Library, Dublin; the British Theatre Institute Library, London; and the New York Public Library.

Thanks are due to Miss Bea Ramtej for her patience and skill in typing and preparing the final manuscript.

The editor and publishers wish to thank the following who have kindly given permission for the use of copyright material:

Constable & Co Ltd for the extract 'Synge and MacKenna' from *Journal and Letters of Stephen MacKenna* by E. R. Dodds (1936).

Contemporary Review for the article on John M. Synge by John Masefield from *Contemporary Review*, Apr. 1911.

James Duffy & Co Ltd for the extract from 'An "Un-Irish" Play' from *The Splendid Years: Recollections by Maire Nic Shiubhlaigh. As told to Edward Kenny* (1955).

Harper & Row Publishers, Inc., for the extract 'An Excitable Man' from *Conversations with James Joyce* by Arthur Power.

Hutchinson Publishing Group Ltd for the extracts from *My Life Story* by Arthur Lynch.

Irish Independent Newspapers Ltd for the extracts from 'John M. Synge: A Personal Appreciation' by D. J. O'Donoghue; 'Abbey Theatre Scene' from the *Evening Telegraph*, Jan. 1907; 'Mr. Synge Beaming' (Author and Mr. Yeats interviewed) from the *Evening Herald* and the *Irish Independent*, 1 Feb. 1907.

The Irish Press Ltd for the extract from 'Synge and the Early Days of the Abbey' by Sean O'Mahony Rahilly in the *Irish Press*, 21 Apr. 1949.

The *Irish Times* for the extract from J. M. Synge: 'I Don't Care a Rap' from the *Dublin Evening Mail*, 20 Jan. 1907.

Macmillan Publishing Co. Inc., for 'My Memories of John Synge' from *The Road Round Ireland* by Pádraic Colum © 1926, renewed 1954 by Pádraic Colum, and the extract from the poem 'Deidre' from *Collected Plays* by W. B. Yeats, copyright 1934 and 1952. Reprinted by permission of the

publishers and A. P. Watt & Son on behalf of M. B. Yeats and Miss Anne Yeats.

J. C. Medley & R. G. Medley for the extract from 'J. M. Synge' from *English Review*, 1914.

John Murray Publishers Ltd and A. M. Heath & Co Ltd for the extracts 'An Exciting Experience' and 'Memories of John Synge' from *Scholars and Gypsies: An Autobiography* by Walter Starkie.

Mrs. Marianne Helweg Rodgers for the extract from a script on J. M. Synge broadcast in May 1952 and reprinted in *Irish Literary Portraits*, BBC, 1972.

Colin Smythe Ltd and the Lady Gregory Estate for the extract from 'Our Irish Theatre' from the Coole Edition of Lady Gregory's Works, reprinted by permission of the publisher and Oxford University Press Inc., N.Y.

The Society of Authors as the literary representative of the estate of James Stephens for the extracts from *Reminiscences of J. M. Synge, James, Seumas & Jacques: Unpublished Writings of James Stephens*.

Southern Illinois University Press for 'Synge in Hospital' from *Joseph Holloway's Abbey Theatre. A Selection from His Unpublished Journal* edited by Robert Hogan and Michael O'Neill. Copyright © 1967 by Southern Illinois University Press. Reprinted by permission of the publisher.

M. B. Yeats, Miss Anne Yeats and Macmillan Publishing Co. Inc., New York, for 'First Meeting with Synge' and 'The Death of Synge' from *Autobiographies* by W. B. Yeats, © 1924 by Macmillan Publishing Co. Inc., renewed 1952 by Bertha Georgie Yeats, and for 'J. M. Synge and the Ireland of his Time' from *Essays and Introductions* by W. B. Yeats, © Mrs. W. B. Yeats, 1961.

M. B. Yeats and Miss Anne Yeats for 'A Memory of Synge' by W. B. Yeats, as printed in the *Irish Statesman*, 5 July 1924, and 'With Synge in Connemara' by Jack B. Yeats.

The publishers have made every effort to trace the copyright holders but if they have inadvertently overlooked any they will be pleased to make the necessary arrangements at the first opportunity.

A Memory of Synge*

W. B. YEATS

A correspondent has sent me the following little essay with the comment 'A short time ago I read Synge's life, and it seemed to me rather lacking in the personal touch, so I wrote down these few memories.'[1] Where we have so little with that 'touch,' I am grateful as an old friend of Synge's, and I have asked the IRISH STATESMAN to put the essay into print that it may remain for some future biographer. John Synge was a very great man, and in time to come every passing allusion that recalls him, whether in old newspaper articles or in old letters, will be sought out that historians of literature may mould, or try to mould, some simple image of the man. Even before the war, invention had begun, for a tolerably well-known American journalist, who had never been under the same roof with Synge, or even set eyes upon him, published scenes and conversations, that were all, from no malicious intention but because of his gross imagination, slander and travesty. He based all upon what he supposed the inventor of so many violent and vehement peasants must be like, knowing so little of human character that he described, without knowing it, Synge's antithesis. I have left my correspondent's notes as they came from her unpractised hand, trivial and important alike. That praise of Wordsworth, for instance, is nothing in itself. To say that 'Wordsworth is more at one with Nature' than some other, is too vague to increase our knowledge, but it recalls some early work of Synge's,[2] certain boyish reveries, that I excluded from his collected edition but not from material that his biographers might use, in which he described minutely brook or coppice—I have forgotten which—a shadowed, limited place, such as children love. I had not known of his passion for Wordsworth, and to know it completes the image. Then again, his liking for Patrick Street has reminded me that a little before his death he planned to make it the scene of a play. I remember that 'little house' in Paris;[3] it was one room which cost him two or three francs a week, yet was not in a slum, but had its own front door and even, I think, some kind of little hall between the front door and room door, and was at the top of a decent house full of flats near the Luxembourg. Paris, as an old astrologer said to me once, is a good town for a poor man, or so it was twenty years ago. I do not know why I have not crossed out that allusion to *Dana*,[4] a very short-lived but delightful paper . . . 'too remote from the world of thought,' except that it might give pleasure to *Dana's* embittered editor. C.H.H. has

* *The Irish Statesman* (Dublin) II, no. 17 (5 July 1924) 530–2.

lent me the photograph she speaks of, but the IRISH STATESMAN has no means of publishing such things. It shows a face less formed and decisive than the face of later years.

NOTES

Synge's first mature love was Cherrie Matheson (1870–1940). His friendship with her was a significant experience at a formative period of his life. Just as he was to capture the brilliance and poignancy of his love for Molly Allgood in the lyricism of *Deirdre of the Sorrows*, so too he preserved the frustrations of his early love for Cherrie Matheson in his first play, *When the Moon Has Set*. Synge, who wrote a disguised account of his love affair with Cherrie Matheson in his *Étude Morbide*, saw her frequently when in Ireland and corresponded regularly with her while in France. He made his first formal proposal of marriage to her in a letter sent on 3 June 1896. It is significant that though he knew her well, he was too shy to propose in person, but wrote instead. His proposal, however, was refused, and in 1902 Cherrie married an Irish schoolteacher, Kenneth Hobart Houghton, and went to live in South Africa. In 1924 she wrote her memoir, signed it with the initials 'C. H. H.', and sent it to W. B. Yeats. The poet was pleased to receive the memoir and wrote two letters to its author. See Ronald Ayling, 'Synge's First Love: Some South African Aspects', *Modern Drama*, VI, no. 4 (Feb 1964) 450–60.

1. Ironically, as David H. Greene and Edward M. Stephens pointed out in *J. M. Synge 1871–1909* (New York, 1959), Cherrie's memoir is a 'rather impersonal reminiscence'; it certainly gives no hint that there was any degree of intimacy between them or that the subject of the article was ever deeply in love for a period of several years with its author. See references to Cherrie Matheson in Edward Stephens. *My Uncle John; Edward Stephens's Life of J. M. Synge*, ed. Andrew Carpenter (London: Oxford University Press, 1974).

2. Synge began to write verse in a decidedly Wordsworthian strain. In his early piece, 'Prelude'—the very title of which is reminiscent of Wordsworth—the kinship with wild Nature rises to an almost extra-human pitch. But in his sonnet, 'Glen Cullen' (1893), Synge perhaps still more distinctly appears as a kind of Irish Lake poet. Wordsworth was still Synge's favourite poet in 1894, and Synge's enthusiasm for his work was shared by Cherrie Matheson [C. H. Houghton].

3. Synge went to Paris in 1894 to teach English and to study at the Sorbonne. He first met W. B. Yeats there on 21 December 1896.

4. *Dana; A Magazine of Independent Thought* (Dublin) was published from May 1904 to April 1905. Among its contributors were W. B. Yeats, Oliver St John Gogarty, Pádraic Colum, George Moore, Edward Dowden, Seamus O'Sullivan, And AE [George Russell]. It was edited by Frederick Ryan and John Eglinton. Frederick Ryan was an Irish writer of nationalist tendencies who became secretary to the Irish National Society in 1903. His play *The Laying of the Foundations* was produced in 1902. For a note on John Eglinton see p. 104.

John Synge as I Knew Him*

C. H. H[OUGHTON]

I first met John Synge in the Autumn of 1896, or perhaps it was 1897.[1] His people asked me to stay with them at Castle Kevin,[2] Annamoe, Co. Wicklow. He was then about twenty-six, a strongly-built man with a rather thick neck and large head, a wonderful face with great luminous sad eyes, and though he was tanned from being constantly out of doors, there was a sort of pallor on his face that gave it a look of delicacy belying his figure, which was that of a hardy mountaineer.

He had just returned from Germany, and it seemed to me then that on account of his good ear for music he had acquired a guttural way of speaking which made him seem almost foreign. When he was interested he spoke with the greatest rapidity. He told us a good deal of his visit to Germany, and was, I remember, collecting roots of ferns to send to some people there who had been kind to him.

We were a very happy little party at Castle Kevin that September: Mrs. Synge and her two sons, and a niece[3] of hers who was a girl friend of mine and had asked me to stay especially for sketching, of which we were both very fond. Looking back on that time after all these years the place seems bathed in autumn sunshine, with a smell of honey from the heather, and a glint of dragonflies' wings in the half-wild garden where we often sat.

As a rule during the day we saw little of the two young men, who used to go off early with a few sandwiches to fish in the little mountain tarns or walk the hills which were then covered with heather or gorse, but in the evenings John Synge used to join us; sometimes we walked in an old avenue of lime trees where there was a constant hum of bees overhead; sometimes we went to the old ruined Castle Kevin which was in the grounds not far from the more modern house, and there we used to watch the sunset. That was the time for talk, and John Synge used to expand and discuss Art and Poetry.

I remember his saying to me he preferred Wordsworth to any other English poet; he said he was more at one with Nature. I also remember his quoting those lines 'The light that never was on sea or land, the inspiration and the poet's dream' as we stood looking at the sunset. He said there was a purity and simplicity about Wordsworth's poetry that appealed to him strongly. Then he talked about Art and told me he loved Corot's[4] work, and later one day in Dublin, he took me to see a little gem of his, which was

---

* *The Irish Statesman* (Dublin) II, no. 17 (5 July 1924) 532-4.

in a loan collection. It was pale greys and golds—very delicate—and I remember thinking at the time that the same man who loved Wordsworth would also love Corot.

Sometimes while we were sketching out in the woods near Castle Kevin we would hear him playing his violin like some fairy fiddler, and one afternoon in the drawingroom he played for me a lovely wild melody of his own. While he was playing he lost himself absolutely in the music, and once or twice he groaned while playing. His small nephew,[5] who was in the room, said when he had finished: 'Uncle Johnnie, why did you make that noise.' He turned to me with a look of agony on his face. 'Oh, did I,' he said, and picked up his violin and quickly left the room. I did not see him again for hours.[6] He told me that he had thought of taking up music as a profession, but his master in Dublin told him he could never make a success of it on account of his extreme nervousness.

I spent ten days at Castle Kevin, and during that time we became good friends, and when they returned to Kingstown,[7] where we were all living at the time, and curiously enough in the same terrace within a few doors of each other, we met frequently. Sometimes we went to the National Gallery or some picture exhibition; sometimes to sit for an hour in St. Patrick's Cathedral and just drink in the beauty of the dear old place. I remember so well the light from the stained glass streaming in on the tattered banners of the old Knights of St. Patrick. He liked that part of Dublin more than the modern part, and especially Patrick Street, which runs between the two Cathedrals, and was then more like some queer continental street with little booths all down the centre of it.

Sometimes he talked about religion. He told me that it was on account of the way a certain clergyman treated one of his congregation that he first felt disgusted with orthodox religion.[8] This good lady whom we both knew had for years been his best church worker, and had a large class for girls, and was really a splendid woman and a most devout Christian. She came into touch with the Baptist Community, and felt she ought to be baptized, and was so, but did not wish to leave her own church or her work; but her clergyman thought otherwise, and literally turned her out of everything, and even cut her in the street. I remember John Synge's wrath as he shouted: 'that man calls himself a Christian!'

The next winter he went to Paris for the first time. From there he wrote me long letters[9] telling about his life, his hardships, and experiences. Though he had hardships I don't think he minded them much; they were all more or less of an adventure. He said the weather was bitterly cold, so he used to stay in bed to keep warm. It was the only way. Also he said his landlady's servant warned him not to eat the meat, and told him it was cat's meat. That amused him very much. These letters were closely written in a small, pointed hand, and often misspelt.[10] Sometimes he began a word in the middle, as if he were thinking much faster than he could write. He told me that one day he was in the Louvre and went into that little room

where the Venus de Milo is. He found a young man there sobbing on the floor—the beauty of the statue had quite overwhelmed him.

After his return from abroad we again met frequently, and he told me a good deal about his time in Paris. He had fallen in love with it, and said Ireland seemed stagnant after the life there. He said: 'It is very amusing to me coming back to Ireland to find myself looked upon as a Pariah, because I don't go to church and am not orthodox, while in Paris amongst the students I am looked upon as a saint, simply because I don't do the things they do, and many come to me as a sort of Father Confessor and wish they could be like me.'

I forget if it was after that first visit to Paris or later that he told me he had met Mr. W. B. Yeats for the first time. I remember asking him if he was a friend of his—he smiled one of his rare illuminating smiles and said: 'You know he is far removed from me, but I think it would not be presumption in me to say he is my friend.' He also spoke of Lady Gregory,[11] and told me I should read her plays, that I would love them. He spoke of having met Miss Maud Gonne[12] at Irish meetings,[13] and that she looked like a tragedy queen, and when she spoke of the wrongs of Ireland she was like one possessed. He was interested in those meetings, but when he found that they were prepared to go any length to gain their ends, he felt he must drop out. He was not an extremist, though he told me he was immensely proud that his grandfather was one of the 'Twelve Righteous Men,' having refused a peerage at the time of the Union. He gave me his photograph about this time. I think it was taken in Paris. It is exactly like him as I remember him. He is sitting, his head thrown rather back, his hand firmly holding a stick, and there is that far-away, sad look in his eyes.

Shortly after this he was walking with me one evening in Dublin and I remember his saying: 'I am a poor man, but I feel if I live I shall be rich; I feel there is that in me which will be of value to the world.' At this time he was writing a good deal, and shortly afterwards went to the Aran Islands. After that I only saw him a few times. Once after his return from Aran he said: 'Oh, I wish you could go there, you would love the Island people.'

Somewhere about this time he had an operation on his throat and looked very delicate.[14] I saw him not long after, and he said to me: 'I tried to send you a telepathic message just before I went under ether. Did you get it?' I had not. He looked disappointed and sad.

Shortly after I went to France, and on my return I did not see him so frequently, as in the meantime I had become engaged to be married. During one little chat we had I remember his saying: 'You know I am getting quite a swell; I have a little house of my own now in Paris.' I told him I had seen him there walking with a friend when I was driving with my father on the opening day of the 'Salon,' where we had been to see the pictures. He seemed much interested, and asked me to describe the person he had been with. I could not do that, but I remember the glimpse I had of

himself so well in his Capuchin cloak, with his head turned towards the man he was with, speaking rapidly all the time.

In 1902 I was married, and came out to South Africa, and in 1904 we went home for a short trip, when I saw him for the last time. I remember we talked a little about *Dana*[15] (a very short-lived but delightful paper). He said it was too good to get a paying circulation in Ireland, that Ireland was too remote from the world of thought.

I have read little of the man as I knew him in any of his published biographies or in articles about him, and I have written these few memories of one who always addressed me in his letters as 'My dear Friend,' as I thought that they might interest some who have only known him in his writings.

NOTES

For a note on C. H. H[oughton] see previous piece—W. B. Yeats, 'A Memory of Synge'.

1. This could not possibly have been in 1897, as Synge proposed to her formally in a letter dated 3 June 1896. Synge had already been in love with her, but she was not aware of it. Cherrie went to stay at Castle Kevin at the end of July 1894. See Edward Stephens, op. cit. p.8

2. After his father died in 1872, Synge's summer holidays were usually spent with his family in Wicklow, sometimes in a rented house at Greystones (then a small fishing village) about fifteen miles south of Dublin. On other occasions they rented houses further inland. One of these was Castle Kevin House, near Annamoe, Wicklow. Synge mentions the name in 'The People of the Glen'. Cf. also 'A Landlord's Garden in County Wicklow'; 'A stone's throw from an old house where I spent several summers in County Wicklow . . .' ; and the Preface to *The Playboy of the Western World*: 'The old Wicklow house where I was staying . . .'

3. Florence Ross (1870–1949), daughter of Mrs Synge's sister and Cherrie's close friend. It was Florence Ross, Synge's childhood companion, who first introduced Cherrie to him. Synge never expected his relations to understand his work. Of all of them, only his cousin Florence ever went to the theatre.

4. Jean-Baptiste-Camille Corot (1796–1875), French painter, noted primarily for his landscapes, who inspired and to some extent anticipated the landscape painting of the Impressionists.

5. Edward Stephens (1888–1950), who later entered the legal profession and had an eventful and distinguished career in Irish public life; after acting as a secretary to the committee which drew up the Irish constitution, he became assistant registrar to the Supreme Court, and finally registrar to the Court of Criminal Appeal. He wrote a biography of Synge which was, in effect, the social history of the Synge family. Some—but a very small portion—of it went into *My Uncle John*, op. cit.

6. Synge's version of the incident, and of the crisis he had gone through with Cherrie, is embodied in a collection of verses he wrote during this visit of Cherrie's. Some years later, when he was able to look back on the incident as closed, he collected these poems under the title *Vita Vecchia* and connected them by short links of prose narrative in which he told the story of his affair by disguising personalities and real events.

7. Now Dun Laoghaire.

8. Cherrie could not accept the religious differences between her and Synge—she and her family were Plymouth Brethren; Synge a non-believer—and refused his proposals of marriage.

9. Synge's correspondence with Cherrie has completely disappeared.

10. Synge's spelling had been spoilt by reading Elizabethan literature; but the defect was also hereditary. He spelt 'cradel'; and if one spelt the words to him, he would go as far as to mistake 'crime' for 'cat' and 'devolution' for 'demonstration'. A significant spelling error was his chronic inability to spell 'changeling' correctly in his letters to Molly Allgood.

11. Lady Isabella Augusta Gregory (1852-1932), Irish dramatist who, with W. B. Yeats and others, aided in founding the Irish National Theatre Society. For many years she was a supporter of the Abbey Theatre, acting as its Director; *Our Irish Theatre* (1913) tells of her early work there. For it she wrote many short plays which blend poetry with a gentle irony. Among her best are *Spreading the News* (1904), *Hyacinth Halvey* (1906), *The Rising of the Moon* (1907) and *The Workhouse Ward* (1908). See Yeats's comments on her in his *Autobiographies* and in various poems such as 'Coole Park, 1929', 'Coole Park and Ballylee, 1931', 'The Municipal Gallery Revisited' and 'Beautiful Lofty Things'. See also Elizabeth Coxhead, *Lady Gregory; A Literary Portrait*, 2nd ed., revised and enlarged (London: Secker and Warburg, 1966); Ann Saddlemyer, *In Defence of Lady Gregory, Dramatist* (Dublin: Dolmen Press, 1966); and Hazard Adams, *Lady Gregory*, (Lewisburg, Pennsylvania: Bucknell University Press, 1974).

12. Maud Gonne (1866-1953), Irish patriot and philanthropist who was engaged in constant political agitation against the British. W. B. Yeats proposed to her but was turned down, and in 1903 she married Major John MacBride, who was executed after the Easter Rebellion in 1916. She was the heroine of many of Yeats's lyrics and plays. See Maud Gonne MacBride, *A Servant of the Queen* (London: Gollancz, 1938); Elizabeth Coxhead, 'Maud Gonne', *Daughters of Erin* (London: Secker and Warburg, 1965) pp. 17-77; A. G. Stock, 'The World of Maud Gonne', *Indian Journal of English Studies*, VI (1965) 56-79; and Chris Healy, 'Maud Gonne', *Confessions of a Journalist* (London: Chatto and Windus, 1904) pp. 227-36.

13. Maud Gonne had founded a Paris branch of the Young Ireland Society known as L'Association Irlandaise.

14. In the autumn of 1897 Synge's hair suddenly began to fall out, and a large lump formed on the side of his neck. His doctor prescribed ointments for his scalp and surgery for the 'enlarged gland', as it was described. It was the first manifestation of Hodgkins Disease, or lymphatic sarcoma, which was to kill him. On 11 December he entered the Mount Street Nursing Home and was operated on. In a short piece entitled 'Under Ether', written soon after the operation but not published until after his death, Synge described his experiences in the nursing home and his sensations under anaesthesia. A second operation was performed in 1907. During that year, Synge also suffered the first indications of a tumour in his side.

15. See previous article—W. B. Yeats, 'A Memory of Synge'.

Synge and MacKenna*

E. R. DODDS

With Synge and with Lynches the newcomer[1] established a fast friendship. Lynch and MacKenna were men of oddly similar stamp: each was a journalist with the interests and the gifts of a scholar and the temperament of a mediaeval knight errant; Lynch was presently to fight for the freedom of the Boers, as MacKenna for the freedom of the Greeks; they were to die within a few days of each other, both of them voluntary exiles from the country they loved best, and neither was to leave on the world a mark proportionate to his ability. Synge and MacKenna on the other hand made, in appearance, a strange pair, the one shy, silent and morose, the other a born talker; but they had in common an ironic humour, a passionate interest in the problem of style, and an unresting curiosity about

---

* 'Memoir', *Journal and Letters of Stephen Mac Kenna* (London: Constable, 1936) pp. 11-13.

the secrets of religious experience. Of their alliance Lynch wrote many years later, 'The man who knew Synge best was Stephen MacKenna, and Synge's first book bears evident marks of MacKenna's influence, or, as I should say perhaps, MacKenna's active help. Stephen MacKenna had himself pushed modesty and diffidence to a higher extreme than Synge, and we have but the scattered fragments of one capable of achieving enduring fame. Little of his imagination and delicate spirit remains except the recollection in a few minds of conversation, the richest, the most charming, at times the most wonderful, I have ever heard.'[2]

MacKenna himself repudiated the suggestion that he had given Synge 'active help.' 'We were the most intimate of comrades,' he wrote,[3] 'and talked days and nights through, and mainly on literature and the technique of it; but except for *The Aran Isles* and his critical work for some London journal—*The Speaker*, I think—I never knew what he had on the loom. He often read me an isolated sentence from the sheet on his Blick[4]—often an entire day's work—but I never knew where the sentence fitted. I did know, curiously, a good deal about his unpublished work; I imagine because he never intended it for publication. He gave me once an immense wad of his verse to read and return; we never spoke of it; I have wondered what he did with it.' In a private letter to Lynch of about the same date he remarks, 'Synge used to get, I remember, very angry when I disliked something which he liked; I think, however, he often accepted the adverse judgement, tacitly.'

Both Synge and MacKenna were distressingly hard up. 'How do those two young men live?' said an inquisitive person. 'Oh, Synge lives on what MacKenna lends him, and MacKenna lives on what Synge pays him back.' Synge in fact lived on an annuity of some £40 a year, which he endeavoured with little success to supplement by free-lance journalism. MacKenna's 'Paris Letter' brought him fifteen shillings a week; and to this he presently added a 'Rome Letter' which he compiled in the rue d'Assas out of newspaper cuttings and a fertile imagination. It was not enough. Synge is reported as looking 'ghastly' at this time from under-nourishment, and MacKenna used to say that he owed to Lynch (who would ask the two to supper as often as he decently could) 'his almost weekly rescue from starvation.' It seems likely that both men laid in these years the foundations of future ill-health.

But, poor as he was, MacKenna was not too poor to help the destitute. Prowling one night on the Seine embankment he fell into talk with one of the homeless men who sleep on the benches there. His new acquaintance proved to be an Armenian doctor, by name Elmassian,[5] whose socialist activities had made him a refugee. MacKenna loved men who preferred their conscience to their comfort: he took the Armenian home, gave him bed and board, and assisted him to pursue his studies at the Pasteur Institute. The refugee became in the end a distinguished bacteriologist; he became also a fast friend both of MacKenna and of Synge, and contributed

some interesting material to Bourgeois' life of the latter.[6] He died in 1913 as director of the Bacteriological Institute of Paraguay.

In the spring of 1897 war broke out between Greece and Turkey. The sympathies of the world were strongly on the side of the Greeks. One evening in April, MacKenna came with Synge to the Café Harcourt to dine with the Lynches, Maud Gonne, and some other Irish folk. The party were sitting out of doors with their glasses, engaged in *conspuer les Turcs*,[7] when a mob of students, similarly engaged, swept past them down the Boulevard St. Michel, closely follwed by the police, who were laying about them with their batons. To escape their blows the Irish party jumped on chairs and tables and pressed tight against the plate-glass windows of the café. Synge, less agile or more obstinate than the rest, received a heavy stroke on the head; but with characteristic reticence he let fall no word on the matter, and it was only when MacKenna had taken him home that he was discovered to be bleeding profusely.[8]

NOTES

Stephen MacKenna (1872–1934), the extreme Irish Nationalist and translator of *Plotinus*, for which he was awarded a gold medal by the Royal Irish Academy in 1924 but which he refused to accept for political reasons. E. R. Dodds wrote a Foreword to this translation, which W. B. Yeats described as worthy at its best to take its place among the masterpieces of English prose. In the winter of 1896–7 MacKenna was offered a small post as Paris correspondent of an English Catholic journal and embraced the chance with joy. His friend Richard Best, whom he had met first at the Irish Literary Society, was already established in Paris, and the two young men occupied adjacent rooms in the rue d'Assas. Through Best and through the branch of Young Ireland, which Maud Gonne had created, MacKenna soon became intimate with the small Irish colony. It was an interesting group of writers, journalists and conspirators: besides Maud Gonne herself, it included the old Fenian, John O'Leary, Arthur Lynch (then Paris correspondent of the *Daily Mail*) and his wife, and J. M. Synge. See Ann Saddlemyer, ed., 'Synge to MacKenna: The Mature Years', *Irish Renaissance*, ed. David Clark and Robin Skelton (Dublin: Dolmen Press, 1966) pp. 65–79.

1. Stephen MacKenna.
2. Arthur Lynch, 'Synge', *The Irish Statesman* (Dublin) xi, no. 7 (20 Oct 1928) 131.
3. Stephen MacKenna, 'Synge', *The Irish Statesman* (Dublin) xi, no. 9 (3 Nov 1928) 169–70.
4. Blickensderfer, Synge's typewriter.
5. Michel Elmassian, whose complete ignorance of English obliged Synge to practise his French.
6. See references to Michel Elmassian in Maurice Bourgeois, *John Millington Synge and the Irish Theatre* (London: Constable, 1913) pp. 16, 42.
7. Spit upon the Turks.
8. Mrs Lynch is Dodd's authority for this incident, of which Maurice Bourgeois in *John Millington Synge and the Irish Theatre* gives a rather different account.

In the Temple of Fame*

ARTHUR LYNCH

Another Irish character, who has found a niche in the temple of Fame, was a resident in Paris in those days and also, though not a very convinced Nationalist, a member of the little Society who sometimes met at Maud Gonne's. This was J. M. Synge, the dramatist. At that time he was little known anywhere, even in Paris. He did not speak French well, and his English, though not that of an Englishman, had no distinctive Irish accent, and he was not then acquainted with the Irish language and the Irish idioms which afterwards he studied so effectively. He had not yet shown the particular qualities which made his reputation, so that on the whole he passed comparatively unnoticed.

Certainly Synge did not cut a great swathe in Parisian life, for he lived in a little *logement*[1] under the roof in the Rue d'Assas, in the Luxembourg Quarter, on forty pounds a year. That already was a feat which showed exceptional character. I think he had his *logement* for about the equivalent of six pounds per annum, and that, with coffee and roll to the good. At that time, as I have already explained, it was possible to get an excellent *déjeuner*[2] at less than one shilling; and as Synge bought eggs now and then and made his own tea, what with modest wants and a patient temperament, he pulled through happily and even allowed himself various mild amusements. I was friendly enough with him,—in fact he has been good enough to remember it, for he has inserted in the 'Playboy of the Western World' an allusion[3] to myself; yet whether due to my intellectual blindness, or to his own modesty, I cannot say, but at that time he gave me no suggestion at all that he was likely to do anything remarkable in literature.

He was a man of giant frame, but untrained and unathletic, so that he looked simply big and awkward; he had a huge head, surmounted by a shock of dark hair, but neither the features nor the countenance were in anyway remarkable. His voice had a flatness of utterance, as of a mild foghorn and, as far as was possible with his great frame and that look of his as if of a being from another civilisation, Synge had always a quiet and somewhat effaced manner. Certainly, it is true, once or twice I was told: 'You ought to speak more to Synge—he is the shrewdest of the lot.'

One little story I remember which shows his quality: We sallied out in the evening, Synge of the party, while the French students were

* *My Life Story* (London: John Long, 1924) pp. 148–50.

demonstrating in favour of Greece. Having been to the East I was by no means quite sure of that choice; but when I remembered the deal of the Sultan with the German Emperor I no longer hesitated. We all joined in and we marched along the Boulevard St. Michel singing 'Conspuez—les—Turcs—Conspuez—les—Turcs—Conspuez!' chanting this solemnly and with great musical conviction.

This demonstration was not to the liking of the French authorities, and they resolved to clear us all out of the Boulevard. During a lull of the demonstration we had taken seats at the Café d'Harcourt, near the corner of the Rue Champollion, when suddenly a compact body of police came like a Macedonian phalanx wheeling round and then charging directly down the pavement. There was only time to spring into the café through open door or through the windows, when that phalanx came along sweeping away everything in its path. A moment's delay might have meant manslaughter and, as they swept by, one of the ladies whom I had been trying to usher into a place of safety cried, in a palpitating voice: 'Let's g-g-get a-away now! We've s-s-seen the b-b-best of the fun!'

I saw Synge standing pale and trembling. I put this down to nervousness at the time. He said nothing. It was only months afterwards that I learned that he had been struck on the back of the head by one of the police, and the blow had been so violent as almost to have knocked him senseless. So far from having shown the white feather, he had brought a Spartan spirit into play, for he uttered no complaint, but had held himself together with desperate force, so as not to cause pain to the ladies.

NOTES

Arthur Lynch was a member of the Irish colony in Paris in Synge's day. An expatriate journalist, he was helping Maud Gonne publish her newspaper *Irlande Libre*.
1. Lodging; accommodation.
2. Lunch.
3. Lynch was Colonel of the Irish Brigade No. 11 on the Boer side during the South African War (see his article 'En Campagne avec les Boers', *Revue de Paris*, 1 Oct 1900). Synge has immortalised him in the first act of *The Playboy of the Western World*, in which Philly says: 'Maybe he went fighting for the Boers, the like of the man beyond, was judged to be hanged, quartered and drawn. Were you off east, young fellow, fighting bloody wars for Kruger and the freedom of the Boers?' The allusion has nothing to do with the play; Synge simply brought it in in memory of his friendship with Lynch, who later as an M.P. referred to his acquaintance with Synge in his speech on the theatre in the House of Commons in April 1913.

Synge*

ARTHUR LYNCH

To the Editor of the IRISH STATESMAN.

DEAR SIR,—A copy of the IRISH STATESMAN of 29th September has been sent to me, and I find that it contains an interesting article on Synge by Sean O Faolain, but there are one or two sentences which are based on erroneous impressions. As Synge has already become an historical person, perhaps you will permit me to dot the i's in places in which reference has been made to the little community of Irish people in Paris, of which Synge was one. I knew Synge before the Boer War, but I do not recollect ever seeing him after my return from South Africa to France, so that the mention—'Colonel Arthur Lynch home from fighting the British in South Africa'—is not quite in order.

Subsequently Synge, in his *Playboy*, has thrown in a reference,[1] which I take to be a token of our former friendship.

Synge is described in the article, quoting from Mr. Yeats, in a manner that I find difficult to appreciate. When I knew him he suffered rather from undue diffidence. With his huge frame, and enormous head, he seemed hardly to belong to the somewhat decadent world of these later days, and in recognition of this fact he had a modest and even gentle and pleading air. It was difficult to get him to speak at all, that is to say, in the sense of 'holding the floor,' but his quiet remarks were often shrewd and surprisingly critical.

The man who knew him best was Stephen MacKenna, and Synge's first book bears evident marks of MacKenna's influence, or as I should say perhaps, MacKenna's active help.

One minuscule point in Sean O Faolain's article is alone sufficient to show a certain remoteness from the scene; he spells Stephen MacKenna as 'Stephen McKenna,'[2] but this is the style and title of another writer much better known, presumably much more popular, but with nothing whatever of that special genius which distinguished our Stephen. They have only one thing in common, they both hate to be misspelt!

Alas, Stephen MacKenna had himself pushed modesty and diffidence to a higher extreme than Synge, and having persisted in that unfortunate mood we have but the scattered fragments of one capable of achieving enduring fame. Little of his imagination and delicate spirit remains except

* *The Irish Statesman*(Dublin) XI, no. 7 (20 Oct 1928) 131.

the recollection in a few minds of conversation, the richest, the most charming, at times the most wonderful, I have ever heard.

It is wrong to speak of 'young Stephen McKenna and his wife' in this connection, for the gracious lady who joined her life to his had in those days not yet appeared above the horizon. Stephen MacKenna wrote to me afterwards, and said that as he was starting on his honeymoon he heard the newspaper boys calling out the news of my sentence to death, and with his ever kind and sympathetic nature that news affected him more than I permitted it to disturb me.

The visits of Willie [W.B.] Yeats and John O'Leary[3] were very infrequent, to our regret at that time. The reference to 'Maud Gonne, then one of the most beautiful women in Europe,' may be allowed to stand without emendation, but I do not think it right to speak of 'their little conspiratorial societies in Paris.' If there were conspiratorial societies in our midst I knew nothing of them myself, for my one great object in Irish affairs was the establishment of the Republic of Ireland—and never at any time have I wavered in that faith—and I believed that the surest way of accomplishing that purpose was boldly holding up before the Irish people the Republican Standard.

Synge was, I believe, only mildly Nationalist. I cannot speak with certainty on this point, for although he was a visitor at our house, I seem to have no recollection of having ever discussed politics with him, and it is from Mrs. Lynch that I have had the suggestion that Synge was critical rather in respect to our means of action than to our ultimate aim. He certainly did not lack courage or even a stoic quality, as appears from a story which, on my evidence, M. Bourgeois has incorporated in his book on Synge.[4]

Finally, to complete these notes, I should make reference to the impression that Synge's *Playboy* made on a French mind. One of our friends was an old French lady, a daughter of Louise Colet,[5] and on our recommendation she went to see the *Playboy*. She was a woman of the world, well acquainted with the modern drama, and endowed with a pretty wit of her own, but I shall never forget the bewilderment, the veritable *ahurissement*[6] with which she listened to the unfolding of Synge's dramatic story. For once she was completely disconcerted and 'thrown out of her hinges.'

Finally, will you permit me, though out of sympathy with your aims, to offer tribute to the ability and the interest of the IRISH STATESMAN.—Yours faithfully,

ARTHUR LYNCH.

NOTES

For a footnote on Arthur Lynch see p. 11.
  1. See previous memoir—Arthur Lynch. 'In the Temple of Fame', p. 11.

2. Stephen McKenna (1888–1967), English novelist; author of *The Reluctant Lover* (1912), *Sonia* (1917), *The Education of Eric Lane* (1921), *Tales of Intrigue and Revenge* (1924), *Due Reckoning* (1927), *Happy Ending* (1929), *Magic Quest* (1933), *A Life for a Life* (1939).

3. John O'Leary (1830–1907) turned to revolutionary journalism under the influence of Davis; edited *The Irish People*; was arrested in 1865 in the great wake of Fenian arrests, and sentenced to twenty years' imprisonment but served only nine; exiled, he chose Paris for a home until allowed to return to Ireland in 1885.

4. See Maurice Bourgeois, *John Millington Synge and the Irish Theatre* (London: Constable, 1913) p. 23.

5. Louise Colet (1810–76), French poet and novelist, as noted for her friendships with leading men of letters as for her own work.

6. Bewilderment; confusion; perplexity.

Synge*

STEPHEN MACKENNA

To the Editor of THE IRISH STATESMAN.

DEAR SIR,—Lest a legend arise, I feel obliged to correct a suggestion made in the letter of my dear friend, Arthur Lynch, in the I.S. of 20th October. I never gave Synge 'active help' in any of his works; we were the most intimate of comrades and talked days and nights through, and mainly on literature and the technique of it; but except for the Aran Isles and his critical work for some London journal—*The Speaker*, I think—I never knew what he had on the loom. He often read me an isolated sentence from the sheet on his Blick—often an entire day's work—but I never knew where the sentence fitted. I did know curiously a good deal about his unpublished work; I imagine because he never intended it for publication; he gave me once an immense wad of his verse to read and return; we never spoke of it; I have wondered what he did with it?

As regards political interest, I would die for the theory that Synge was most intensely Nationalist; he habitually spoke with rage and bitter baleful eyes, of the English in Ireland, though he was proud of his own remote Englishry; I take it he wanted as dearly as he wanted anything, to see Ireland quite free; but one thing kept him quiet—he hated publicity, co-operation and lies.

He refused to support the Gaelic League[1] because one pamphlet it issued contained the statement (I indicate roughly) that to know modern Irish was to be in possession of the ancient Saga. The lying that gathered round the political movement seemed to him to soil it utterly, and all that had part in it; he tolerated my political activities, intense in desire though petty in effect, only because he knew that I never uttered the modish lie

* *The Irish Statesman* (Dublin) XI, no. 9 (3 Nov 1928) 169–70.

and only just failed to expose it; in sum I'd say he was exactly as John O'Leary,[2] that princely gentleman, that noble soul, that flaming, ineffective lover of Ireland and of Irish freedom. The two were not friends, but they were in many ways identities. All good wishes.—Yours faithfully,

STEPHEN MACKENNA.

NOTES

For a note on Stephen MacKenna see p. 9.
1. The Gaelic League was formed in 1893 to revive Irish language and culture.
2. For a note on John O'Leary see p. 14.

First Meeting with Synge*

W. B. YEATS

I am certain of one date, for I have gone to much trouble to get it right. I met John Synge for the first time in the autumn of 1896, when I was one-and-thirty, and he four-and-twenty. I was at the Hôtel Corneille instead of my usual lodging, and why I cannot remember, for I thought it expensive. Synge's biographer says that you boarded there for a pound a week, but I was accustomed to cook my own breakfast, and dine at an Anarchist restaurant in the Boulevard St. Jacques for little over a shilling. Some one, whose name I forget, told me there was a poor Irishman at the top of the house, and presently introduced us. Synge had come lately from Italy, and had played his fiddle to peasants in the Black Forest—six months of travel upon fifty pounds—and was now reading French literature and writing morbid and melancholy verse. He told me that he had learned Irish at Trinity College, so I urged him to go to the Aran Islands and find a life that had never been expressed in literature, instead of a life where all had been expressed. I did not divine his genius, but I felt he needed something to take him out of his morbidity and melancholy. Perhaps I would have given the same advice to any young Irish writer who knew Irish, for I had been that summer upon Inishmaan and Inishmore, and was full of the subject. My friends and I had landed from a fishing-boat to find ourselves among a group of islanders, one of whom said he would bring us to the oldest man upon Inishmaan. This old man, speaking very slowly, but with laughing

* Extracted from 'The Tragic Generation', *The Trembling of the Veil* (London: T. Werner Laurie, 1922) pp. 157-222; reprinted in *Autobiographies* (London: Macmillan, 1955) pp. 343-6.

eyes, had said, 'If any gentleman has done a crime, we'll hide him. There was a gentleman that killed his father, and I had him in my own house six months till he got away to America.'

From that on I saw much of Synge, and brought him to Maud Gonne's, under whose persuasion, perhaps, he joined the 'Young Ireland Society of Paris', the name we gave to half a dozen Parisian Irish, but resigned after a few months because 'it wanted to stir up Continental nations against England, and England will never give us freedom until she feels she is safe', the one political sentence I ever heard him speak. Over a year was to pass before he took my advice and settled for a while in an Aran cottage, and became happy, having escaped at last, as he wrote, 'from the squalor of the poor and the nullity of the rich'. I almost forget the prose and verse he showed me in Paris, though I read it all through again when after his death I decided, at his written request, what was to be published and what not. Indeed, I have but a vague impression, as of a man trying to look out of a window and blurring all that he sees by breathing upon the window. According to my Lunar parable, he was a man of the twenty-third Phase; a man whose subjective lives—for a constant return to our life is a part of my dream—were over; who must not pursue an image, but fly from it, all that subjective dreaming, that had once been power and joy, now corrupting within him. He had to take the first plunge into the world beyond himself, the first plunge away from himself that is always pure technique, the delight in doing, not because one would or should, but merely because one can do.

He once said to me, 'A man has to bring up his family and be as virtuous as is compatible with so doing, and if he does more than that he is a puritan; a dramatist has to express his subject and to find as much beauty as is compatible with that, and if he does more he is an aesthete', that is to say, he was consciously objective. Whenever he tried to write drama without dialect he wrote badly, and he made several attempts, because only through dialect could he escape self-expression, see all that he did from without, allow his intellect to judge the images of his mind as if they had been created by some other mind. His objectivity was, however, technical only, for in those images paraded all the desires of his heart. He was timid, too shy for general conversation, an invalid and full of moral scruple, and he was to create now some ranting braggadocio, now some tipsy hag full of poetical speech, and now some young man or girl full of the most abounding health. He never spoke an unkind word, had admirable manners, and yet his art was to fill the streets with rioters, and to bring upon his dearest friends enemies that may last their lifetime.

No mind can engender till divided into two, but that of a Keats or a Shelley falls into an intellectual part that follows, and a hidden emotional flying image, whereas in a mind like that of Synge the emotional part is deadened and stagnant, while the intellectual part is a clear mirror-like technical achievement.

But in writing of Synge I have run far ahead, for in 1896 he was but one picture among many. I am often astonished when I think that we can meet unmoved some person, or pass some house, that in later years is to bear a chief part in our life. Should there not be some flutter of the nerve or stopping of the heart like that MacGregor Mathers experienced at the first meeting with a phantom?

John M. Synge: A Personal Appreciation*

D. J. O'DONOGHUE

The death of J. M. Synge, at a comparatively early age ('the fatal thirty-seven') will come home with double force to those who had the pleasure of his acquaintance. Without exaggeration (of which there has been a good deal in this connection), it can be said that a very potent personality has passed out of the literature of our time. It is not so much by what he has done as by what he would undoubtedly have achieved had he lived, that the loss to letters is so considerable. Personally, I fancy that his brooding genius would have concentrated itself to far greater purpose than his comparatively small literary output suggests. But we have yet to see the poems[1] and the tragedy on the subject of 'Deirdre,'[2] which he left unpublished.

A FAMOUS HOTEL

My own acquaintance with him began about ten years ago. In a letter I received from W. B. Yeats in the year 1899, just as I was about to start for Paris, the latter called my attention to the fact that in the hotel[3] where I always stayed there was then living 'an Irishman named Synge,' who was well worth knowing, and who was anxious to meet fellow-countrymen with literary tastes. Yeats had just returned from his first visit to France. Like many other Irishmen, he stayed at a small hotel in the Rue Corneille, opposite the Odeon Theatre, which has an interesting history, too long to narrate here. It has been somewhat transformed internally of late years, but externally and, indeed, in other particulars, it still remains the Bohemian resort it used to be. Readers of 'Trilby'[4] will recall that it was the hotel of Little Billee. It was for many years the residence of John O'Leary and other notable Irishmen, and it was to the veteran patriot's recommendation that I, like Yeats and others, owed our knowledge of its

* *The Irish Independent* (Dublin) (26 Mar 1909) p. 4.

existence. Synge was living at the time on a very small annuity, so small that he had to deny himself many things which he wanted badly, and it has often occurred to me that possibly his subsequent failure of health may have arisen from the hardships he underwent in those struggling days. As it happens, I did not meet him on the occasion of the 1899 visit, for he had left the hotel for a small room near by, where he was able to make more of his slender means than in any hotel, however moderate.

LIFE IN PARIS

As was the general custom with students, he furnished his small room (in a house in the Rue d'Assas facing the Luxembourg Gardens) by a few purchases in the Montparnasse quarter, and there lived his rather lonely life for several years, broken only by his yearly visit to the Aran Islands, where he was studying Irish at possibly its purest source. I met him in Paris in the following year, and sat for many hours each day with him in his little room or in a small neighbouring cafe, talking over the possibilities of literary life, and perhaps building castles in the air, a pastime than which no career offers more opportunities to the optimist. When talk lagged Synge would take down his violin, one of his few consolations, and play over many mournful Irish airs, melodies which appealed to his somewhat sad nature. Then as always, though a most charming and kindly companion, and Irish of the Irish in his sympathies, his outlook was a little morbid and decidedly cosmopolitan. He had been wandering about the Continent for some years, chiefly in Germany, Italy, and France, and had endeavoured to make himself acquainted with the literatures of those countries. His natural taste led him rather to the decadent writers, and possibly this may account for certain manifestations of his later work. He was anxious to become a writer, and with true perception, thought his best chance was to try and write about a people whom he liked and of whom he thought the world knew too little. So he began to record his impressions of the Aran Islands. Years before it was published I read his book on the West with great interest, greatly admiring the style and wondering at what appeared to me the exotic point of view of the writer.

LITERARY BEGINNINGS

Meanwhile, with the aid of his small income, and an occasional cheque from the 'Speaker' for reviewing Gaelic publications, Synge worked on, frequently in very poor health, slowly elaborating everything he wrote, for writing was very laborious process to him. He found it difficult to obtain congenial literary work, and, therefore, contented himself with a faint hope that some day he might find his opportunity. While awaiting that desired opening, he lived strictly within his means, sought no amusements, and found his only pleasure in meeting his friends and talking over literary and art matters with them. He had gained honours in Trinity College, had passed most successfully through the Royal Irish Academy of Music, and

had read well, if not widely. He appeared to be older, as well as stronger, than he really was. Few, looking at his apparently robust frame and masculine features, would have believed him delicate, and his grave and careworn look added years to his age in the opinion of his friends. He had succeeded, after hard study in mastering the Irish language, a fact in itself which was creditable to his Irish feeling, for he belonged to a family historically opposed to Irish aspirations, from the several Archbishops and Bishops[5] of the name in the seventeenth and eighteenth centuries down to most recent times. His small library largely consisted of Irish authors, but his thoughts were not, perhaps, with them.

THE DRAMATIC MOVEMENT

It was the rise and development of the Irish drama that gave Synge his chance of distinguishing himself. He was deeply interested in the revival, for he felt, what everyone must admit, that he had a natural dramatic instinct, and a grip on the serious realities of life. His 'Shadow of the Glen,'[6] which many critics likened to the ancient legend of the Ephesian Matron, but which always suggested a chapter in Voltaire's 'Zadig' to me, came with something of a shock to those who did not expect the new movement would ever graft an alien point of view on essentially universal human emotions, and the new dramatist was severely blamed. 'Riders to the Sea'[7] convinced his most hostile critics, however, that Synge was a force to be reckoned with. Whether the essential idea of a play was or was not disagreeable, it was seen that here was a writer who could poignantly burn it into an audience. Then, after this powerful appeal to the emotional side of humanity, there came the play which, more than anything else, made its author famous.

THE 'PLAYBOY'

The now historic commotion over this play is too recent to call for much comment. But one or two things it is important to remember. Unlike some of his more furious partizans, Synge himself was the last man in the world to complain of popular dislike of his themes or his treatment of them. He readily recognised with the generous feeling which was his prevailing characteristic, that this was no personal matter, and that his audiences (however wrong-headed from his point of view, in their misconception of his purpose) were unquestionably able to discriminate between the man and his work. The rapturous applause which was lavished on his 'Riders to the Sea,' performed with the 'Playboy,'[8] was proof positive that the audiences were sincere in their dislike. Synge certainly objected to be shouted down, but he never expected any Irish audience to receive his 'Playboy' with delight. Some years before Yeats had declared that 'the battle of the future in drama would be fought round Synge.' There was an element of truth in the observation, which seemed at the time wild enough in its extravagance. I do not think Synge loved the glare and crash of the

battle, his essentially kindly and modest nature shrinking from such publicity. It cannot be said that he unduly forced himself on anyone, nor do I believe he ever wished anybody else to thrust him too prominently before the public. Now that the smoke of the battle has lifted to some extent, even those whose outlook on Irish life was not the same, will regret the death of a notable Irishman, while his friends will always deplore the disappearance of one of the most engaging and delightful personalities of our time.

NOTES

David James O'Donoghue (1866–1917), Irish literary figure and friend of Synge who later became Librarian of University College, Dublin. It was from Synge that O'Donoghue first heard the well-known story of how Baudelaire, in order to startle the public (*epater le bourgeois*), once called on Maxime du Camp with his hair dyed green. O'Donoghue's writings on Synge include 'The Synge Boom: Foreign Influences', *Irish Independent* (Dublin) (21 Aug 1911) p. 4; 'John M. Synge', *Irish Book Lover* (Dublin and London), III, no. 2 (Sep 1911) 31; and 'John Millington Synge', *The Poets of Ireland: A Biographical and Bibliographical Dictionary of Irish Writers of English Verse* (Dublin: Hodges Figgis; London: Oxford University Press, 1912) p. 448.

   1. Synge's poems were published in *Poems and Translations* (Churchtown, Dundrum: Cuala Press, 1909).
   2. *Deirdre of the Sorrows* was published by Cuala Press in 1910.
   3. Hotel Corneille.
   4. *Trilby*, then just published (1894) by the Anglo-Parisian artist and writer, George du Maurier.
   5. The Synges were strongly enough devoted to their faith to produce five bishops and a quantity of other clergy and missionaries over the years since the first Synge came to Ireland in the seventeenth century.
   6. For a note on *In the Shadow of the Glen* see p. 25.
   7. *Riders to the Sea* was first produced by the Irish National Theatre Society at the Molesworth Hall, Dublin on 25 February 1904.
   8. For a note on *The Playboy of the Western World* see p. 36.

An Excitable Man*

JAMES JOYCE

One evening we had an argument about the merits of Synge. Joyce knew him when he was living in the Rue d'Assas but found him very difficult to get on with.

—He was so excitable, Joyce told me. I remember once going around to him and suggesting that we should spend the 14th July in the Parc de St

* Arthur Power, *Conversations with James Joyce* (London: Millington, 1974) pp. 33–4.

Cloud. But Synge objected violently to the idea of spending the holiday, as he expressed it, 'like any bourgeois picnicking on the grass', and he refused to go. In fact there were such heated arguments between us that in the end I had to give up seeing him.

—And what do you think of his work? I asked.

—I do not care for it, he told me, for I think that he wrote a kind of fabricated language as unreal as his characters were unreal. Also in my experience the peasants in Ireland are a very different people from what he made them to be, a hard, crafty and matter-of-fact lot, and I never heard any of them using the language which Synge puts into their mouths.[1]

—But he must have got it from somewhere, I said. I know that in the west of Ireland I used to hear marvellous phrases. I remember once asking a peasant on Costelloe Bay if there were many seals in it. 'Seals', he exclaimed, 'sure they do be lying out there as thick as the fingers of my hand, and they sunning themselves on the rocks'—a phrase which seemed to me to be pure Synge. And do you remember the speeches of Mary Byrne in *The Tinker's Wedding*[2] when she talks about the great queens and they making matches from the start to the end, 'and they with shiny silks on them the length of the day, and white shifts for the night'?

—Now who ever heard talk like that? protested Joyce.

—The question is, I said, is literature to be fact or is it to be an art?

—It should be life, Joyce replied, and one of the things I could never get accustomed to in my youth was the difference I found between life and literature. I remember a friend of mine going down to stay in the west, who, when he came back, was bitterly disappointed—'I did not hear one phrase of Synge all the time I was down there', he told me. Those characters only exist on the Abbey stage. But take a man like Ibsen—there is a fine playwright for you. He wrote serious plays about the problems which concern our generation.

NOTES

Born in Waterford, Ireland and educated in Hampstead, England, Arthur Power moved with his family to France when he was fourteen years of age. He fought in World War I, and on release from the army at the end of the war he went, via Florence, Rome and Pisa, to Paris where he first met James Joyce and his family in the early twenties. A well-known artist, he now lives and works in Dublin. Synge met Joyce for the first time in 1903. (In a letter to Harriet Weaver on 8 November 1916 Joyce was inaccurate when he dated their first meeting 1902.) Synge showed him the manuscript of *Riders to the Sea*, but Joyce, who later admired the play and translated it into Italian, pronounced it un-Aristotelian. Synge was annoyed, they spent the rest of the time arguing, and Synge's 'harsh gargoyle face' was subsequently enshrined in *Ulysses*. Joyce was twenty years old at the time, only six months out of college, and his prospects were far grimmer than Synge's. They saw more of each other after Joyce returned to Dublin in April, though Synge records in his diary only one other meeting, on 21 September 1903.

1. In 1912, Joyce went to the Aran Islands and wrote two articles on them for the *Piccolo della Sera*. 'The articles display none of the contempt for Irish rural life and folklore which he had evinced in 1902 and 1903 in talking with Yeats and Lady Gregory; as he predicted in "The Dead", Joyce came round to sharing Ireland's primitivism. He depicted Aran with the

affection of a tourist who has read Synge, noted the peculiarities in the islanders' dialect, and described curious local customs and history.' —Richard Ellmann, *James Joyce* (1965) p. 336.

2. *The Tinker's Wedding* was first presented by the Afternoon Theatre at His Majesty's Theatre, London, on Thursday, 11 November 1909.

An 'Un-Irish' Play*

MAIRE NIC SHIUBHLAIGH

We returned to Dublin flushed from our victory and not a little awed by the high praise which had been showered upon us; our visit had brought us into personal contact with many of the most eminent figures in the London theatre world. We had, it seemed, arrived. Who was to blame us if we thought it was but a mere step to even greater triumphs? But any hopes we had were soon dashed. Our next appearance in Dublin could not compare in any way with the popular success of the London one. In October, just five months after our return, we introduced a new play by an author whose work was later to make the name of the Irish theatre famous all over the world, and had the unusual experience of turning a powerful nationalist club in Dublin against us.

The play, a first attempt, was entitled *In the Shadow of the Glen*.[1] The author was an obscure journalist named J. M. Synge.

It was early in June, 1903, that Lady Gregory called us to her rooms at the Nassau Hotel and read Synge's play over to us. The piece was a one-act comedy based on an Irish folk-tale the author had heard from an old Aran Island seanachie[2]—the story of the aged husband feigning death to test his youthful wife's fidelity; denouncing her, but forgiving her lover. The plot, strictly speaking, was not original, but the treatment was. It was completely different to anything we had known before; the play itself was a masterpiece of dramatic construction. It was, in fact, the first of the Irish 'realist' dramas, and the quiet young man who sat unobtrusively in the background while Lady Gregory read aloud his words, was to take his place amongst the greatest dramatists the Irish theatre produced.

John M. Synge who came to us with his play direct from the Aran Islands, where the material for most of his later works was gathered, was born near Dublin in 1871, graduated at Trinity College, and shortly afterwards left Ireland for the Continent, living alternately in Germany and France, where he made a rather precarious livelihood as a violinist and contributor to literary magazines. Yeats had discovered him in Paris about

* *The Splendid Years: Recollections of Maire Nic Shiubhlaigh, As Told to Edward Kenny* (Dublin: James Duffy, 1955) pp. 39–43.

1897[3] and, recognising the quality of his writings, had brought him back to Ireland, where he introduced him to Aran, prophesying that in the beautiful lyrical prose of the western peasant he would find an original vehicle for dramatic composition. He was right. Synge went to Aran for a month, and stayed there, on and off, for a matter of years. He drew his inspiration from the hearths of the tiny whitewashed cabins and the harsh rocks of the western seaboard, gathering tales and expressions from the old and the young of the most picturesque portion of Ireland. In a short life—he died at the early age of thirty-eight—he wove them into sombre dramatic tapestries, embroidered with the rhythmic language of the true Irish peasant. His prose, highly musical and enriched with flashes of the most beautiful poetry, he devised simply by transcribing direct from the Gaelic of the islands. It is most difficult for an actor to master; most effective if delivered correctly.

He was a gentle fellow, shy, with that deep sense of humour that is sometimes found in the quietest people. His bulky figure and heavy black moustache gave him a rather austere appearance—an impression quickly dispelled when he spoke. His voice was mellow, low; he seldom raised it. But for his quiet personality he might have passed unnoticed at any gathering. During rehearsals of his play, he would sit quietly in the background, endlessly rolling cigarettes. This was a typical gesture, born more of habit than of any desire for tobacco—he gave away more cigarettes than he smoked. At the first opportunity, he would lever his huge frame out of a chair and come up on to the stage, a half-rolled cigarette in each hand. Then he would look enquiringly round and thrust the little paper cylinders forward towards whoever was going to smoke them. In later years he became the terror of fire-conscious Abbey stage-managers. He used to sit timidly in the wings during plays, rolling cigarettes and handing them to the players as they made their exits.

He could speak wisely and constructively of his own work. 'All art is a collaboration,' he later wrote in a preface to his *Playboy of the Western World*, 'and there is little doubt that in the happy ages of literature, striking and beautiful phrases were as ready to the story-teller's or the playwright's hand as the rich cloaks and dresses of his time. . . . In Ireland, those of us who know the people have the same privilege . . . on the stage one must have reality and one must have joy, and that is why the intellectual drama has failed and people have grown sick of the false joy of the musical comedy that has been given them in place of the rich joy found only in what is superb and wild in reality. In a good play every speech should be as fully flavoured as a nut or an apple, and such speeches cannot be written by anyone who works among people who have shut their lips on poetry. . . . '

Synge was a genius, one of the great literary figures of his time, but brilliance often ripens under the most difficult conditions. *In the Shadow of the Glen* was sufficiently in advance of its time to arouse in Dublin audiences a completely unfounded indignation. Its production raised a storm of

protest in some sections of the Press[4] that was stupid and ridiculous, disconcerting its unfortunate author, and amazing most of us, who had never looked upon the play as anything but an exceptionally well-written comedy.

Indeed, from my point of view as an actress, there was nothing wrong with *In the Shadow of the Glen* at all. Though it looked—and was—a difficult play to interpret, each of the four characters offered ample scope to whoever would be chosen to play them. But there was a division of opinion against it within the society. Dudley Digges, our juvenile lead, was of the opinion that it was an unsuitable piece for us to play, and he was joined in this by some other members who said that they would be compelled to withdraw from the society if it was put on. As it had already been decided to produce the play, there was nothing to be done but let them go. Dudley resigned with three or four others, taking with him Maire Quinn, who later became his wife. He was, of course, missed. Digges, an old and well-liked member, was the most polished young actor the society had, and without him our organisation was incomplete. It was many years before the vacancy created by his withdrawal was filled. Happily, however, for him, his resignation did little to affect his career. Soon after he left us, he had an offer to appear in Irish plays at the St. Louis American Exhibition of 1903. Here, playing opposite Maire Quinn, he rapidly ascended to leading parts on Broadway, where he worked for many years. Afterwards he went into films—he was probably the first of the 'Irish players' to do so—living between Hollywood and New York until his death.

With Maire Quinn gone, I was cast as Nora Burke, the young wife in the new play. I found the part a difficult one to master for it was completely unlike anything that I or anybody else in the company had ever played previously. At first I found Synge's lines almost impossible to learn and deliver. Like the wandering ballad-singer I had to 'humour' them into a strange tune, changing the metre several times each minute. It was neither verse nor prose. The speeches had a musical lilt, absolutely different to anything I had heard before. Every passage brought some new difficulty and we would all stumble through the speeches until the tempo in which they were written was finally discovered. I found I had to break the sentences—which were uncommonly long—into sections, chanting them, slowly at first, then quickly as I became more familiar with the words. Neither Fay nor Synge offered me much help during rehearsals. I found it difficult to understand this until Fay explained that I had been chosen specially for the part because of my comparative inexperience as an actress. 'When you *read* a book or a play you supply your own characters. The author just makes suggestions which you, the reader, enlarge upon. If you were a more experienced actress you might read into this part something which, perhaps, was never intended. Be the *mouthpiece* of Nora Burke, rather than Nora Burke. You will be corrected only if you are inaudible or if your movements are wrong.'

To our surprise, the attitude of those who had left the society was echoed on a larger scale by some sections of the public and the Press even while Synge's play was still in rehearsal. The piece was 'un-Irish', wrote some reviewers, an 'insult' in fact to the peasant women of Ireland whom Nora Burke was taken to typify. There was an immense verbal furore about it. A number of writers claiming that Synge was slyly attacking the institution known as the 'made marriage',[5] and attributing it solely to Ireland, raised all sorts of objections. Others wrote of the character of Nora Burke: 'Nora Burke is a lie.' Of the play they said: 'It is no more Irish than the Decameron. It is a staging of the old-world libel on womankind—the Widow of Ephesus.'[6]

NOTES

In 1903 William G. Fay's Irish National Dramatic Company developed into the Irish National Theatre Society, whose first President was W. B. Yeats. The company's modest headquarters were the Molesworth Hall, Camden Street, Dublin. Eight plays were produced, two of which—*In the Shadow of the Glen* and *Riders to the Sea*, performed on 8 October 1903 and 25 February 1904, respectively—were the work of J. M. Synge, who made there a fairly successful debut. *In the Shadow of the Glen*, which is a bitter sketch of the loveless marriages of the Irish country-folk, was based on a folktale which Synge had heard on the Aran Island in 1898. However, it was hissed on the opening night, produced a hot controversy in the papers, and its performance led to something of an internal crisis in the affairs of the Irish National Theatre Society, Maud Gonne having resigned on account of it.

1. *In the Shadow of the Glen* was first produced at the Molesworth Hall, Dublin, on Thursday, 8 October 1903, with George Roberts as Dan Burke, Maire Nic Shiubhlaigh [Maire Walker] as Nora Burke, P. J. Kelly as Michael Dara, and W. G. Fay as the Tramp. It was presented together with W. B. Yeats's *On the King's Threshold* and *Kathleen ni Houlihan*.
2. Story-teller.
3. Synge first met Yeats on 21 December 1896.
4. For a record of the press reviews of *In the Shadow of the Glen* see E. H. Mikhail, *J. M. Synge: A bibiliography of Criticism* (London: Macmillan, 1975) pp. 108–9.
5. As AE [George Russell] pointed out in 'Religion and Love', *Dana* (Dublin) (1904) p. 45, the Irish peasant girl 'will follow her four-legged dowry to the house of a man she may never have spoken twenty words to before her marriage'.
6. In a letter to the Editor of the *United Irishman* (Dublin) (11 Feb 1905) p. 1, Synge said that his play 'differs essentially from any version of the story of the Widow of Ephesus with which he was acquainted '. The play was developed from a story told to Synge by Pat Dirane, the old shanachie of Inishmaan, in 1898. This story, in a somewhat polished version, was included in Synge's *The Aran Islands* (1907). See the original draft of the story in Synge's *Collected Works*, III, ed. Ann Saddlemyer (London: Oxford University Press, 1968) pp. 254–6.

In the Shadow of the Glen*

WILLIAM G. FAY

Looking back on it all, I can hardly believe how quickly events marched in 1903. It was truly our *annus mirabilis*.[1] We had begun it in a dire poverty that made us the laughing-stocks of Dublin, and you have to be a Dubliner to know how cruel that was. In those first days we were made to feel the force of the ancient sage's words that the hardest thing about poverty is that it makes people laugh at you. Yet within six months of our beggarly beginnings we had performed in London and been acclaimed as masters and pioneers in our art by all the most eminent critics. In the autumn we revealed an Irish dramatist, whose work now belongs not to Ireland but to the world, and discovered the greatest Irish actress since Peg Woffington; and, to crown all, Miss Horniman[2] paid her first visit to Dublin.

The actress was Sara Allgood,[3] then a mere girl, who came to us to play the Princess Buan in Mr. Yeats's new play, *The King's Threshold*,[4] which was to be part of our autumn programme. We had one other new item, called *In the Shadow of the Glen*. The author's name, John Millington Synge, conveyed nothing to us or anybody else at that time. All we knew was that he was a Wicklow man, a graduate of Trinity College, whom Mr. Yeats had discovered a few years before in Paris, living pretty miserably by odds and ends of reviewing and now and then fiddling in an orchestra. Mr. Yeats had told him that he would never do any good in Paris. If he wanted to make a name in letters, as he apparently did, let him pack off to the Aran Islands and study the stuff of life there; and with surprising docility off Synge packed. Thenceforward Aran was his home. He seems to have found life there interesting rather than enjoyable, and it is doubtful if either his spirit or his body could have borne it had he not been able to spend a substantial part of each year in Paris. However, it was in Aran that he found his *métier*, as Mr. Yeats had prophesied. *In the Shadow of the Glen* was his first effort, but it showed little sign of the 'prentice hand. It was a peasant play, but oh, how different from any of our other peasant pieces! It was the first of the modern Irish realistic plays. From beginning to end there was not a syllable of sentiment. The dialect used was entirely strange to us, which was hardly surprising seeing that Synge had invented it himself. His device was the simple enough one of translating practically word for word from Gaelic. It has been imitated often since—notably by

* William G. Fay and Catherine Carswell *The Fays of the Abbey Theatre* (London: Rich and Cowan, 1935) pp. 136–41.

Mr. Caradoc Evans for broad comic effects in his Welsh satires—but it was new then, and to me as producer it presented a serious problem. I was quite at home with the traditional 'stage Irish' of the 'arrah,' 'begob' and 'bedad' school, as well as the stage Irish of O'Keefe,[5] Boucicault[6] and Whitbread.[7] I knew the Irish of Lever and Lover and, what is better and more correct, the dialect used in Carleton's[8] *Traits and Stories of the Irish Peasant*. It was all the more disconcerting for me to encounter an Irish dialect that I could not speak 'trippingly on the tongue.'

The droll thing was that neither could Synge speak it! In time I mastered it, but he never did—perhaps partly because his years abroad had removed every trace of brogue from his speech—though he could always check it when he heard it spoken. He came to Dublin for the rehearsals—a tawny, thick-set fellow with the head of a lion and a terrifying moustache, and looking at least forty though actually he was just turned thirty-two. He and I soon got together and experimented with the dialogue until, after much hard practice, I got at how the speeches were built up, and could say any of the lines exactly in the way he wanted. They had what I call a balance of their own, and went with a kind of lilt: 'she had the lightest hand . . . at making a cake . . . or milking a cow . . . that wouldn't be aisy.' Once I had found out the proper 'tune' I never had any difficulty with the dialect in any of his other plays.

Synge always finished a play in his mind to the last detail before he started writing it down, and once it was on paper he could not alter it. I remember asking him once if he did not think that a certain speech might be improved. He replied, 'I quite agree, but these were the words he used and I only set them down.' He told me that as the play came into being in his imagination the characters took on a life of their own and said and did things without consulting him at all. It is a fact that you cannot cut a line in any of his plays without damaging the whole structure. His power of visualisation was perfect. I would work out a scale plan of the stage and furniture, and he would say, 'That is just the way I saw the room as I was writing the play.' It was very lucky that there seemed to be a sort of pre-established harmony between my mind and his, for I always wanted to produce his plays as nearly as possible as he saw them. If I asked him, 'Was Dan standing where he is on the right, behind the table, when he said these lines?' he would say, 'No, he was on the right-hand side of the table with his hand on it.' He was a great joy to work with, for he had a keen sense of humour and plenty of patience, and above all he knew what he wanted, and when he got it said so—which is a virtue very rare in dramatic authors.

It was during his first visit to Inishmaan, the middle Island of Aran, that old Pat Dirane[9] told him the story of *In the Shadow of the Glen*, relating it as if it had happened to himself one dark night ten miles from Dublin. Who can say where the story came from originally? We afterwards discovered three other versions of it in different parts of the country. Perhaps it is not Irish at all in origin, but a mediaeval folk tale wafted from the Continent to our

shores—for folk tales are like thistledown for travelling—during the Middle Ages. This is suggested by the closing passage of old Pat's version, which ran thus: 'She went into the bedroom, but the divil a bit of her came back. Then the dead man got up and he took one stick; he gave me the other to myself. We went in and saw them lying together with her head on his arm. The dead man hit him a blow with his stick, so that the blood of him leapt up and hit the gallery.' Synge and I were always puzzled to know how that word gallery got into the story. You don't find galleries in Irish cottages, but you might find something of the sort in a peasant's house in the south of Europe. Is the inference that the story came to us from, say, Italy and was being told by the country folk in the days of Boccaccio?

In the Shadow of the Glen provoked a hurricane of abuse which, bad as it was, was no more than a foretaste of what was in store for us and the author in later days and was to attain the most extravagant heights of foolishness and violence with the production of *The Playboy of the Western World*. The treatment meted out to Synge during his lifetime might well have stirred the rest of the world to wonder if Irishmen really had any sense of humour. A possible explanation of this peculiar obtuseness, this complete inability to appreciate satire except when it is directed at other nations, is that, until our movement forced one upon them, the Gaels never had a theatre of their own and therefore little understanding of the functions and values of the stage. They had not the needful sophistication to accept a play as a play and leave it at that. Instead of being convulsed with laughter at the stark comedy of *In the Shadow of the Glen* they were convulsed with what Oscar Wilde calls 'the rage of Caliban at seeing his own face in the glass.' Of course, as usual, Mr. Yeats had to bear the brunt of the attack, for whatever we did he was sure to get the chief blame, but the rest of us got our fair share. We were told that there were no Irish people like those in Synge's play. Arthur Griffith[10] in the *United Irishman* played us a peculiarly dirty trick. Somehow—by whose treachery or carelessness we never discovered—he managed to get hold of a script, and did not wait for the play to be produced, but opened his attack beforehand. The points of objection taken were—'There are no loveless marriages in Ireland.' 'No one could be found in Ireland like the characters in this play.' 'It is a crude version, pretending to be Irish, of the famous or infamous story of the Widow of Ephesus.' There was a monotonous similarity about all the comments, but I can't help giving one or two more. 'A Boccaccio story masquerading as an Irish play.' 'Men and women in Ireland marry lacking love, and live mostly on a dull level of amity. Sometimes the woman dies of a broken heart, but she does not go away with the tramp.' 'As will be seen, the play is an evil compound of Ibsen and Boucicault.'

It took many years for Ireland to learn—if indeed she has yet learned—that in J. M. Synge she had produced a great dramatist. During all my time the majority of the Irish Press were bitterly hostile and the audiences were not much better.

NOTES

William George (1872–1947) and Frank J. (1870–1931) Fay were Irish actors who were important in the early history of the Abbey Theatre. They began their careers at the Dublin Dramatic School, run by Mrs Lacy, wife of a touring manager. In 1898 they formed the Armonde Dramatic Society. In 1902 the Irish National Dramatic Society included the two Irish actors. Stephen Gwynn, in *Irish Literature and Drama*, says: 'The style of acting identified with the Abbey Theatre is due to the genius of the Fays—and with W. G. Fay especially.' William Fay left the Abbey and went to America in 1908. Synge was especially interested in the staging and rehearsing of the plays produced at the Abbey Theatre. In the former capacity he found a particularly competent collaborator in W. G. Fay, who acted as stage-manager until 1908.

1. Year of wonders.
2. Annie Elizabeth Frederika Horniman (1860–1937), English theatre manager and patron, one of the first to organise and encourage the modern repertory theatre movement. She built and managed the Abbey Theatre in Dublin for the Irish National Theatre Society (1904) and bought and managed the Gaiety Theatre in Manchester (1908–1921). See James W. Flannery, *Miss Annie F. Horniman and the Abbey Theatre* (Dublin: The Dolmen Press, 1970).
3. Sara Allgood was one of the company's leading actresses. She created the parts of Cathleen in *Riders to the Sea*, Molly Byrne in *The Well of the Saints*, Widow Quin in *The Playboy of the Western World*, and the nurse Lavarcham in *Deirdre of the Sorrows*. She is Molly Allgood's sister. See Elizabeth Coxhead, 'Sally and Molly', *Daughters of Erin* (London: Secker and Warburg, 1965) pp. 167–224.
4. *The King's Threshold* was first produced at the Molesworth Hall, Dublin, on 8 October 1903.
5. John O'Keefe (1747–1833), Irish actor and playwright; gained reputation as author of *Tony Lumpkin in Town* (1778).
6. Dion Boucicault (1820(?)–90), Irish actor and playwright. Among his plays are *The Octoroon* (1859), *The Colleen Bawn* (1860) and *The Shaughraun* (1874).
7. J. W. Whitbread, Irish playwright and proprietor of the Queen's Theatre, Dublin. His melodramas, manufactured on the Boucicault model, include *The Irishman* and *Shoulder to Shoulder*.
8. William Carleton (1794–1869), bilingual Irish novelist who was brought up among the Irish peasantry and acquired an insight into their ideas and feelings. His finest work is in his short stories, collected under the title of *Traits and Stories of the Irish Peasantry* (two series, 1830, 1833). He also wrote several novels including *Fardorougha the Miser* (1837), *The Misfortunes of Barny Branagan* (1841), *Valentine M'Clutchy* (1845), *The Black Prophet: A Tale of the Famine* (1847), *Rody the Rover* (1847), *The Tithe Proctor* (1849), *The Squanders of Castle Squander* (1854) and *The Evil Eye* (1860). Carleton fell in love with a Protestant girl, married her, and became a Protestant. He received a pension of £200 a year from the government.
9. 'Pat Dirane', the old story-teller who could tell 'as many lies as four men', was Pat Doran. See Introduction to *The Aran Islands*.
10. Arthur Griffith (1872–1922), Irish political leader; joined Irish Republican Brotherhood; founder and editor of *The United Irishman* (1899); first President of the Irish Free State (1922).

*The Well of the Saints**

WILLIAM G. FAY

And now the Abbey Theatre was launched on its voyage of fame. It was not a rich adventure. We had only a matter of forty pounds in cash in hand to keep us afloat, but, thanks to Miss Horniman,[1] we were worthily housed and free from debt, and could fairly boast of being the only endowed theatre in the English-speaking world. We faced the future with confidence, not to say hardihood, and the measure of it was that for our very next production (February 1905) we trailed our coats in front of the Dublin public by presenting a full-length play by Synge. This was *The Well of the Saints*,[2] in my opinion his best play. He gave himself a large enough canvas on which to paint the picture in his mind. He had felt what all writers of one-act plays must feel sooner or later, that the concentration demanded by a short play allows one to give only the headings and suggestions of what ought to be full scenes, if truthfully developed. As for the story, a great deal of research has gone in trying to find out the source of it; but to me this has always seemed to be a waste of time, though it may be interesting. All good dramatists have taken their plots from where they could find them. Shakespeare used Italian *novelle;* Wilde got the theme of *Lady Windermere's Fan* from *The Family Herald;* and Arnold Bennett, as he once told me, had a box full of old Spanish plays that he dipped into now and again when he was short of ideas. Whether the idea of *The Well of the Saints* came from *The Maid of Malines* or *Marianiela* is immaterial. In any case those who knew Synge knew that in his travels through the back mountains of Wicklow and Kerry, as well as during his sojourn in the Aran Islands, he had collected enough stories for many plays without having recourse to foreign soil.

When one is producing a difficult play like this it is not easy to remain objective, to see it from the point of view the audience will take on the first night. It is only after years of experience with all kinds of plays and all kinds of audiences that one acquires the working knowledge of crowd psychology that enables one to tell, while a play is still in rehearsal, whether it is likely to offend or not. That is the most one can do. There is no way of foretelling success. The most experienced producers and actors can be deceived, and are so every day. But one can at least discern any factor that will militate

* William G. Fay and Catherine Carswell, *The Fays of the Abbey Theatre* (London: Rich and Cowan, 1935) pp. 166–9.

against success and try to eliminate it before the public sees the play. Here, I believe, the author has to be consulted, and authors are notoriously obstinate. I never could get either Yeats or Synge to understand that if you write plays to be acted, not read by the fireside, there are certain rules that you cannot break without destroying the sympathy between the stage and auditorium. The rules I refer to are not technical but psychological. For example, as *The Well of the Saints* took shape, I realised that every character in the play from the Saint to Timmy the Smith was bad-tempered right through the play, hence, as I pointed out to Synge, all this bad temper would inevitably infect the audience and make them bad-tempered too. I suggested that the Saint anyway might be made into a good-natured easy-going man, or that Molly Byrne might be made a lovable young girl, but Synge would not budge. He said he wanted to write 'like a monochrome painting, all in shades of the one colour.' I argued that all drama depended on contrast and on tension. All in vain. We had to agree to differ.

One technical trouble we had to overcome was that Synge had not yet acquired the art of breaking up his dialogue into short speeches, without which it is impossible for the actors to get pace. Many of his speeches were very long. They took a cruel lot of practice before we could get them spoken at a reasonably good pace and without at the same time losing the lovely lilt of his idiom. Take, for example, the Saint's speech at the end of the first act. 'May the Lord—who has given you sight—send a little sense into your head the way it won't be—on you two selves you'll be looking,' etc. Worse still for the actors is Martin's speech in Act III when he enters blind. 'The divil mend Mary Doul—for putting lies on me—and letting on she was grand. The divil mend the ould saint for letting me see it was lies,' etc.

The Well of the Saints had very much the same reception as *In the Shadow of the Glen*. As before, few of our public knew what to make of it. Was it a piece of harsh realism or was there something else behind it? The lyrical speeches were beyond them, and there was the old suspicion that most of the plays we produced were intended in some way to debunk the saintly Irish character. Who, for example, would be trusting Mr. Yeats? Hadn't he always something up his sleeve? If it wasn't the birds of Angus Oge it might be a political rabbit of some kind. Then, Synge, of course, had heard of a man called Boccaccio and a story about the Widow of Ephesus. In short the play was admired and enjoyed by those who were capable of regarding it simply as a play without reading into it a criticism of the Irish people or an attack on their religion. But these were too few. The great majority, thinking of religion and themselves, abominated the play on both counts. It had a bad Press and we lost money and audience over it.

However, we enjoyed doing it, not only because it gave us excellent scope for acting, but also because a three-act play was less of a strain than our usual bill of four one-act plays. Every actor will understand what it means to have to play four short parts in the same evening involving four

changes of costume and make-up in addition to the necessity for rapid emotional readjustment.

NOTES

For a note on William G. Fay see p. 29.
1. For a note on Miss Horniman see p. 29.
2. *The Well of the Saints* had its first production at the Abbey Theatre on 4 February 1905 with W. G. Fay as Martin Doul, Emma Vernon as Mary Doul, Geroge Roberts as Timmy, Sara Allgood as Molly Byrne, Maire Nic Shiubhlaigh as Bride, P. MacShiubhlaigh as Mat Simon, and F. J. Fay as The Saint.

With Synge in Connemara*

JACK B. YEATS

I had often spent a day walking with John Synge, but a year or two ago I travelled for a month alone through the west of Ireland with him. He was the best companion for a roadway any one could have, always ready and always the same; a bold walker, up hill and down dale, in the hot sun and the pelting rain. I remember a deluge on the Erris Peninsula, where we lay among the sand hills and at his suggestion heaped sand upon ourselves to try and keep dry.

When we started on our journey, as the train steamed out of Dublin, Synge said: 'Now the elder of us two should be in command on this trip.' So we compared notes and I found that he was two months older than myself. So he was boss and whenever it was a question whether we should take the road to the west or the road to the south, it was Synge who finally decided.

Synge was fond of little children and animals. I remember how glad he was to stop and lean on a wall in Gorumna and watch a woman in a field shearing a sheep. It was an old sheep and must have often been sheared before by the same hand, for the woman hardly held it; she just knelt beside it and snipped away. I remember the sheep raised its lean old head to look at the stranger, and the woman just put her hand on its cheek and gently pressed its head down on the grass again.

Synge was delighted with the narrow paths made of sods of grass alongside the newly-metalled roads, because he thought they had been put there to make soft going for the bare feet of little children. Children knew, I think, that he wished them well. In Bellmullet on Saint John's eve, when

* In W. B. Yeats, *Synge and the Ireland of His Time* (Dundrum, Dublin: Cuala Press; New York: Mitchell Kennerly, 1911) pp. 39–43. Originally published in *New York Evening Sun*, and condensed in *Irish Nation* (Dublin) 1, no. 33 (14 Aug 1909) 7.

we stood in the market square[1] watching the fire-play, flaming sods of turf soaked in paraffine, hurled to the sky and caught and skied again, and burning snakes of hay-rope.[2] I remember a little girl in the crowd, in an ecstasy of pleasure and dread, clutched Synge by the hand and stood close in his shadow until the fiery games were done.

His knowledge of Gaelic was a great assistance to him in talking to the people. I remember him holding a great conversation in Irish and English with an innkeeper's wife in a Mayo inn. She had lived in America in Lincoln's day. She told us what living cost in America then, and of her life there; her little old husband sitting by and putting in an odd word. By the way, the husband was a wonderful gentle-mannered man, for we had luncheon in his house of biscuits and porter, and rested there an hour, waiting for a heavy shower to blow away; and when we said good-bye and our feet were actually on the road, Synge said, 'Did we pay for what we had?' So I called back to the innkeeper, 'Did we pay you?' and he said quietly, 'Not yet sir.'

Synge was always delighted to hear and remember any good phrase. I remember his delight at the words of a local politician who told us how he became a Nationalist. 'I was,' he said plucking a book from the mantlepiece [sic] (I remember the book—it was 'Paul and Virginia')[3] and clasping it to his breast—'I was but a little child with my little book going to school, and by the house there I saw the agent. He took the unfortunate tenant and thrun him in the road, and I saw the man's wife come out crying and the agent's wife thrun her in the channel, and when I saw that, though I was but a child, I swore I'd be a Nationalist. I swore by heaven, and I swore by hell and all the rivers that run through them.'

Synge must have read a great deal at one time, but he was not a man you would see often with a book in his hand; he would sooner talk, or rather listen to talk—almost anyone's talk.

Synge was always ready to go anywhere with one, and when there to enjoy what came. He went with me to see an ordinary melodrama at the Queen's Theatre, Dublin, and he delighted to see how the members of the company could by the vehemence of their movements and the resources of their voices hold your attention on a play where everything was commonplace. He enjoyed seeing the contrite villain of the piece come up from the bottom of the gulch, hurled there by the adventuress, and flash his sweating blood-stained face up against the footlight; and, though he told us he had but a few short moments to live, roar his contrition with the voice of a bull.

Synge had travelled a great deal in Italy in tracks he beat out for himself, and in Germany and in France, but he only occasionally spoke to me about these places. I think the Irish peasant had all his heart. He loved them in the east as well as he loved them in the west, but the western men on the Aran Islands and in the Blaskets fitted in with his humour more than any; the wild things they did and said were a joy to him.

Synge was by spirit well equipped for the roads. Though his health was often bad, he had beating under his ribs a brave heart that carried him over rough tracks. He gathered about him very little gear, and cared nothing for comfort except perhaps that of a good turf fire. He was, though young in years, 'an old dog for a hard road and not a young pup for a tow-path.'

He loved mad scenes. He told me how once at the fair of Tralee he saw an old tinker-woman taken by the police, and she was struggling with them in the centre of the fair; when suddenly, as if her garments were held together with one cord, she hurled every shred of clothing from her, ran down the street and screamed, 'let this be the barrack yard,' which was perfectly understood by the crowd as suggesting that the police strip and beat their prisoners when they get them shut in, in the barrack yard. The young men laughed, but the old men hurried after the naked fleeting figure trying to throw her clothes on her as she ran.

But all wild sights appealed to Synge, he did not care whether they were typical of anything else or had any symbolical meaning at all. If he had lived in the days of piracy he would have been the fiddler in a pirate-schooner, him they called 'the music—' 'The music' looked on at everything with dancing eyes but drew no sword, and when the schooner was taken and the pirates hung at Cape Corso Castle or The Island of Saint Christopher's, 'the music' was spared because he *was* 'the music.'

NOTES

Jack B. Yeats (1871–1957), younger brother of W. B. Yeats and Ireland's greatest painter. He was also a playwright of originality and importance. His plays include *Apparitions* (1933) and *La La Noo* (1943). He is also the author of a number of idiosyncratic prose works including *Sligo* (1930), *The Amaranthers* (1936) and *The Careless Flower* (1947). A biography of him by Hilary Pyle was published in 1970, and his collected plays and prose were edited by Robin Skelton in 1971. In 1905 C. P. Scott of the *Manchester Guardian* commissioned Synge to do a series of articles on those impoverished areas of the West of Ireland, stretching approximately from the northeast corner of Donegal to the town of Tralee in Kerry, known as the Congested Districts. It was a formidable assignment, and Synge wrote immediately to the parliamentary representative of the district to get the information he needed before starting out on 3 June. The trip, with Jack B. Yeats to draw the sketches, lasted exactly one month.

1. See J. M. Synge, 'At a Wicklow Fair: The Place and the People', *Manchester Guardian* (9 May 1907) p. 12.

2. Synge remembered the same incident when he wrote the lines in which Christy Mahon described his drunken father 'throwing clods against the visage of the stars'.

3. By the French novelist Bernandin de Saint-Pierre (1737–1814).

Synge Watching His Rehearsals*

OLIVER ST JOHN GOGARTY

Then, farther up the town in Camden Street,[1] Synge would be sitting watching rehearsals. He sat silent, holding his stick between his knees, his chin resting on his hands. He spoke seldom. When he did, the voice came in a short rush, as if he wished to get the talk over as soon as possible. A dour, but not a forbidding man. Had he been less competent it might have been said of him on account of his self-absorption that he 'stood aloof from other minds. In impotence of fancied power.' He never relaxed his mind from its burden.

I asked him if he did not intend his 'Playboy' for a satire to show up, for one thing, how lifeless and inert was the country where a man could be hailed as a hero for doing something kinetic even though it were a murder, and how ineffectual, for, as the event showed, even that had not been committed. He gave me a short glance and looked straight in front of himself, weighing me up and thinking how hard it would be to get the public to appreciate his play as a work of art, when one who should know better was reading analogies and satire into it already. He shook my question off with a shake of his head.

* *As I Was Going Down Sackville Street; A Phantasy in Fact* (London: Rich and Cowan, 1937) pp. 283–4; (London: Sphere Books, 1968) pp. 292–3.

NOTE

Oliver St John Gogarty (1878–1957), Irish physician, wit, poet, and novelist; Senator of the Irish Free State (1922–36). An intimate friend of both Yeats and Joyce, he appears in *Ulysses* as Buck Mulligan. His many volumes of poetry include *The Ship* (1918), *An Offering of Swans* (1924) and *Others to Adorn* (1939). In 1937 he published a book of reminiscences, *As I Was Walking Down Sackville Street*, which became the cause of a famous libel action. In 1954 he published his autobiography, *It Isn't This Time of Year at All*.

1. The early headquarters of the Irish National Theatre Society were a modest hall in Camden Street, Dublin.

Abbey Theatre Scene*

This evening a representative of the *Evening Telegraph* called at the Abbey Theatre in order to get Mr. Synge's views on the opposition on Saturday night and last night to his play, 'The Playboy of the Western World.' He there found that, with Mr. W. B. Yeats, he had gone to lunch in the Metropole Hotel; and here he had a conversation with the two[1] gentlemen on the extraordinary situation that has arisen.

* * *

Mr. Synge, asked about the word[2] which caused the uproar on Saturday night towards the close of the play, said it was an everyday word in the West of Ireland, which would not be taken offence at there, and might be taken differently by people in Dublin. It was used without any objection in Douglas Hyde's[3] 'Songs of Connaught,' in the Irish, but what could be published in Irish perhaps could not be published in English!

On the question of the main point of the play, Mr. Synge repeated Mr. Yeats's idea about art being exaggerated, and said that as a fact the idea of the play was suggested to him by the fact that a few years ago a man who committed a murder was kept hidden by the people on one of the Arran Islands until he could get off to America, and also by the case of Lynchehaun,[4] who was a most brutal murderer of a woman, and yet, by the aid of Irish peasant women, managed to conceal himself from the police for months, and to get away also.

* Extracted from *Evening Telegraph* (Dublin) (29 Jan 1907) pp. 3–4.

NOTES

W. B. Yeats drew Synge, who had planned to devote his life to writing critical articles on French writers, into writing about Irish subjects. He urged him, on one of his visits to Paris, to give up France and 'to go to the Aran Islands and find a life that has never been expressed in literature'. In 'The Municipal Gallery Revisited' he says:

> John Synge, I and Augusta Gregory, thought
> All that we did, all that we said or sang
> Must come from contact with the soil

Synge reached the greatest height of comedy in *The Playboy of the Western World*, the fullest and most elaborate of all his works. In this play Christy Mahon, a shy youth, becomes a hero when he reveals that he has slain, as he thinks, his domineering father. He triumphs in the local sports and wins the spirited Pegeen Mike away from her terrified fiancé. However, when Christy's father, Old Mahon, arrives, and Christy tries to kill him again, he loses his glamour as a hero, even with Pegeen. When the play opened on Saturday night, 26 January 1907,

there were riots at the Abbey Theatre. The objections against the play were made on religious, moral and patriotic grounds. On religious grounds, the audience objected that the play's references to God, the Catholic Chruch, and the sacrament of marriage were blasphemous and profane. On moral grounds, the play's attitude to parricide was found to be equivocal and morally indefensible. The third line of attack was that the play was unpatriotic and likely to reflect discredit on Ireland. These objections were raised either by perfectly sincere nationalists or by political coteries. See James Kilroy, *The 'Playboy' Riots* (Dublin: Dolmen Press, 1971) and W. B. Yeats's description of the events in *The Arrow* (Dublin) I, no. 3 (23 Feb 1907).

1. The text of Yeat's interview is reprinted in E. H. Mikhail, *W. B. Yeats: Interviews and Recollections* (London: Macmillan, 1977).
2. The word 'shift' (= chemise; slip).
3. Dr Douglas Hyde (1860–1949), founder of the Gaelic League (1893) and first President of Ireland. He devoted his life to the restoration of the Irish language and culture. His writings include *Folklore of the Irish Celts* (1890), *The Love-Songs of Connacht* (1893), *Beside the Fire* (1898), *A Literary History of Ireland* (1899) and *Legends of Saints and Sinners* (1915). Synge greatly admired the language of Hyde's translations of *The Love Songs of Connacht* and said of his Gaelic play *The Twisting of the Rope* in 1901 that it 'gave a new direction and impulse to Irish drama, a direction towards which, it should be added, the thoughts of Mr. W. B. Yeats, Lady Gregory and others were already tending'. On the influence of Hyde's *The Love-Songs of Connacht* on Synge's *The Playboy of the Western World* see Maurice Bourgeois, *John Millington Synge and the Irish Theatre* (London: Constable, 1913) p. 227. See Diarmuid Coffey, *Douglas Hyde, President of Ireland* (Dublin: Talbot Press, 1938), and Lester Connor, 'The Importance of Douglas Hyde to the Irish Literary Renaissance', *Modern Irish Literature: Essays in Honor of William York Tindall*, ed. Raymond J. Porter and James D. Brophy (New Rochelle, N. Y.: Iona College Press, 1972) pp. 95–114.
4. The Lynchehaun case and the Aran case are both instances of men wanted by the police for murder being given sanctuary by the peasants. James Lynchehaun, who had assaulted a woman on Achill Island and who is mentioned in James Joyce's *Ulysses*, was well known in Ireland because he eventually escaped to America where the British secret service tracked him down in Indianapolis. Irish patriotic organisations, however, interested themselves in his case, and the American courts refused to extradite him on the grounds that he was a political prisoner. Not content with his freedom, Lynchehaun returned to Ireland, visited Achill disguised as a clergyman and got out of the country safely again before the police discovered his presence. Synge was telling the truth and not just bolstering his case, for in one of the earlier drafts of the play one of the minor characters was made to say, 'If they did itself I'm thinking they'd be afeared to come after him. Sure they never laid a hand to Lynchehaun from the day they knew the kind he was.'—David H. Greene and Edward M. Stephens, *J. M. Synge 1871–1909* (New York: Collier Books, 1961) p. 244.

I Don't Care a Rap*

J. M. SYNGE

Playwrights and actors propose; the gods dispose. My intention last night was first to see that very vexatious play, 'The Playboy of the Western World', so that I might be better prepared to have a talk with its author,

* *Dublin Evening Mail* (29 Jan 1907) p. 2.

Mr. J. M. Synge, which was my chief errand. But the gods had willed it otherwise. Technically considered, perhaps they were not gods; they were confined mostly to the left-hand side of the upper end of the house; but they were all-powerful. They overpowered everybody and everything else. Certainly they could not have been anything less than saints; for none but saints could take up the quarrel of virtue with such a vehemence, such an unflagging zeal. After all 'saints' is the better word here. It must not be forgotten that we are dealing here with the National Theatre of a nation of saints.

At any rate, I was cheated out of the play by a band of men who seemed to enjoy their own voices more than all else, though it is difficult to tell why they should have taken the trouble to pay for that. It seemed at times as if the whole affair was all

PRE-ARRANGED BEFOREHAND;

as if those men had come there with the set purpose, whether of their own accord, or inspired by others, to prevent the performance of the play, and they succeeded fully. From the moment Pegeen Mike began to show her partiality to Christopher Mahon, on the strength of his heroics, there was a hissing and booing and stamping and kicking which made one turn one's eyes upwards, to see if the roof was there yet. After some moments Mr. W. G. Fay[1] who played Christopher Mahon, stood up to deliver a harangue, in which he begged the disturbers to withdraw and claim their money back, which would be given them with pleasure. He was severally interrupted with 'Booh! booh!' 'Shame! shame!' 'Not good enough for Liverpool or New York!' 'What would ye say if they brought such a thing from London?' 'We have nothing against the actors, but the play—booh!' 'Call the author—Synge! Synge!' Many others amongst the audience angrily hurled phrases in Irish against Mr. Fay, till in the end, he threatened to

BRING IN THE POLICE.

The curtain was let down, and after a while the police came in. But there is nobody so useless on occasions as the policeman. I counted nine policemen, all in a bunch, right beside the principal disturbers, who carried on just the same as ever; and the nine policemen looked like nine big sticks with helmets on top. The play was resumed, but not a note could be heard from the stage. To look on at the actors and actresses all seemed stupid mimicking. Still they kept it up bravely to the very end, and the bravest part of it all was their coming forward to bow to the audience at the end of each act.

MR. SYNGE INTERVIEWED

Mr. Synge, who had promised me half an hour after the play was over, was scarcely in a mood for being interviewed. He looked excited and

restless, the perspiration standing out in great beads over his forehead and cheeks, and, besides, he seemed just then in extraordinary demand by sundry persons, who had all sorts of things to say to him. I practically had to collar him and drag him away with me to some quiet spot. But the quietest I could find was the narrow passage leading up to the stage from the entrance hall, and that was anything but quiet. We were continually jostled and interrupted, and the draughts, too, were blowing from all directions, but I was not going to grumble. I was conscious of the one thing only—that I had cornered my man, and must have it out with him. Neither was there any time to waste; so I began straight away.

'Tell me, Mr. Synge, was your purpose in writing this play to represent Irish life as it is lived—in short, did you think yourself holding up the mirror to nature?'

'No, no,' Mr. Synge answered, rather emphatically.

That was going in direct opposition to the first rule laid down by the foremost playwright. But another Irish playwright before Mr. Synge has already put Shakespeare to shame, if we are to put our faith in what George Moore said of some of the plays of Edward Martyn; only it may be that not many of us have got this faith.

'What, then, was your object in this play?' I asked after a while.

'Nothing,' Mr. Synge answered, with sustained emphasis, due probably to his excited condition, 'simply the idea appealed to me—it pleased myself, and I worked it up.'

'But do you see now how it displeases others? And did you ever think, when writing it, how it would be received by the public?'

'I never thought of it—Hi!' to one of the attendants, who was brushing past us, 'see the police are there ready to quell the row'—then turning to myself,

'IT DOES NOT MATTER A RAP

I wrote the play because it pleased me, and it just happens that I know Irish life best, so I made my methods Irish.'

'Then,' I interposed, 'the real truth is you had no idea of catering for the Irish National Theatre. The main idea of the play pleased your own artistic sense, and that you gave it an Irish setting as a mere accident, owing to your intimate knowledge of Irish life.'

'Exactly so,' he answered.

I paused for a moment to reflect upon this new tenet in art. In idealistic quarters it has ever been the cry, art for art's sake; here it was, art for the artist's sake. But though it may seem tall talk on the part of the artist who sets up for himself such a standard, in effect it runs the risk often of being but a poor standard.

'But you know,' I suggested, 'the main idea of your play is not a pretty one. You take the worst form of murderer, a parricide, and set him up on a

pedestal to be worshipped by the simple, honest people of the West. Is this probable?'

'No, it is not; and it does not matter. Was Don Quixote probable? and still it is art.'

'What was it that at all suggested the main idea of the play?' I asked.

'Tis a thing that really happened. I knew a young fellow in the Arran Islands who had killed his father, and the people befriended him and sent him off to America.'

'But did the girls all make love to him because he had killed his father, and for that only, the sorry looking bedraggled, and altogether repelling figure though he was personally?'

'No. Those girls did not, but mine do.'

'Why do they? What is your idea in making them do it?'

'It is to bring out the humour of the situation. It is a comedy, an extravaganza, made to amuse—'

At this point

THE LIGHTS WENT OUT

and we were left in complete darkness. For the matter of that, I shall always remain in the dark as to Mr. Synge's ideas on art. I am unable either to appreciate them or grasp them.

Mr. Synge and I presently withdrew to the main hall, where the lights were left undisturbed. But here several people got hold of him, and the thread of our conversation was broken for a time.

After some minutes I managed to regain hold of Mr. Synge, when I summed up the case to him.

'Then, I am to understand, Mr. Synge that your play is not meant to represent Irish life. The fact that a story such as depicted by you actually did happen in a modified way is neither here nor there. Life is not made up of isolated occurrences, but of the things that happen day by day. In fact, you had no object whatever in the play except your own art. The plot appealed to your own artistic sense, and for the rest you did not care.'

'Yes,' he answered, 'and I don't care a rap how the people take it. I never bother whether my plots are typical Irish or not; but my methods are typical.'[2]

His excitement seemed to go on growing, as if somebody had said something to him during the interval to ruffle him still more. He went on talking to me at a rate which made me glad I was not taking him down in shorthand. I cannot believe there is a pencil on earth likely to have kept pace with him then. I was just able to catch him up at the end, to the effect that the speech used by his characters was the actual speech of the people, and that in art a spade must be called a spade.

'But the complaint is, Mr. Synge, that you call it a bloody shovel. Of course, I am not speaking from personal experience, for I have not heard a word at all from the stage, though I could not possibly be nearer it. And

that reminds me, Mr. Synge, what do you propose to do for the rest of the week, in face of what has taken place to-night?'

'We shall go on with the play to the very end, in spite of all,' he answered, snapping his fingers, more excited than ever. 'I don't care a rap.'

NOTES

1. For a note on William G. Fay see p. 29.
2. Synge's own account of what he said in that interview is included in a letter to Stephen MacKenna:

> He—the interviewer—got in my way—may the devil bung a cesspool with his skull—and said, 'Do you really think, Mr. Synge, that if a man did this in Mayo, girls would bring him a pullet?' The next time it was, 'Do you think, Mr. Synge, they'd bring him eggs?' I lost my poor temper (God forgive me that I didn't wring his neck) and I said, 'Oh well, if you like, it's impossible, it's extravagance (how's it spelt?). So is Don Quiote!' He hashed up what I said a great [deal] worse than I expected, but I wrote next day politely backing out of all that was in the interview. That's the whole myth. It isn't quite accurate to say, I think, that the thing is a generalization from a simple case. If the idea had occurred to me I could and would just as readily have written the thing as it stands without the Lynchehaun case or the Aran case. The story—in its *essence*—is probable, given the psychic state of the locality. I used the case afterwards to controvert critics who said it was *impossible.* – Robin Skelton and David R. Clark, eds, *Irish Renaissance* (Dublin: Dolmen Press, 1965) p. 75.

The letter makes it clear that Synge's claim to naturalistic reporting was, in this case as in others, a defensive response to criticism. A letter which Synge wrote to the press as a consequence of the interview is also significant. In a letter to the *Irish Times* on Thursday, Synge tried to dispel the impressions he had himself created by his unfortunate interview in the *Evening Mail*, when he implied that his play was not to be taken seriously. He had wisely kept aloof from the controversy over the play and, as W. B. Yeats afterwards said, he was useless in such situations. Synge explained:

> 'The Playboy of the Western World' is not a play with 'a purpose' in the modern sense of the word, but although parts of it are, or are meant to be, extravagant comedy, still a great deal more that is behind it, is perfectly serious when looked at in a certain light. That is often the case, I think, with comedy, and no one is quite sure to-day whether 'Shylock' and 'Alceste' should be played seriously or not. There are, it may be hinted, several sides to 'The Playboy'. 'Pat', I am glad to notice, has seen some of them in his own way. There may be still others if anyone cares to look for them.—J. M. Synge. Letter to the Editor, *Irish Times* (Dublin) (31 Jan 1907) p. 5.

'Pat' was Patrick Kenny, who had seen the play largely as a prophecy of the downfall of an Ireland that was exporting its strongest inhabitants and being emotionally and spiritually debilitated by the institution of arranged and loveless marriages.

The Author Interviewed*

Mr. Synge, the author of *The Playboy*, stated that it was at his and Lady Gregory's[1] request the police[2] withdrew, their instructions to them being that they were not to interfere unless personal violence was resorted to. They, he said, simply claimed the liberty of art to choose what subjects they thought fit.

* *Evening Telegraph* (Dublin) (29 Jan 1907) p. 2.

NOTES

1. Yeats was absent from Ireland for the début of *The Playboy*; he was lecturing in Scotland. While Lady Gregory resolutely kept the play running against organised interruption, Yeats hurried back to Dublin and arranged a debate in the Abbey Theatre on Monday, 4 February 1907, following the week's performances.

2. The *Evening Telegraph* (Dublin), on 29 January 1907, p. 2. reported:

> After the lapse of a quarter of an hour close on a dozen policemen entered the theatre and took up a position commanding the left side of the pit, whilst another body of constables were stationed outside the building. Their advent was hailed with a torrent of boos. The performance was now resumed . . .
>
> Amidst booing and other conceivable and almost inconceivable noises, the action of the drama was proceeded with . . .
>
> Now the unexpected occurred. As the result of some apparently mystic sign or command, the constables turned right about and marched in stately style out of the building.

Mr. Synge Beaming*

There was comparative calm in the Abbey Theatre last night when 'The Playboy of the Western World' was again produced. The audience was smaller than on any night since the production of the play, which has been received with such a storm of disapproval. The fact that there was little disorder enabled those present to form a more correct impression of the character of the play than could hitherto be gained.

* Extracted from '*The Playboy* Has a Quieter Time at the Abbey, But Two Arrests Were Made; Author and Mr. Yeats Interviewed', *Evening Herald* (Dublin) (1 Feb 1907) p. 5. Also in the *Irish Independent* (Dublin) (1 Feb 1907) p. 5.

MR. SYNGE BEAMING

A few minutes before eight o'clock the pit and balcony were fairly well filled, but there were only a couple of dozens in the stalls. The 'pitites' were manifestly antagonistic to the play. Before the curtain rose on 'Riders of the Sea' [sic] they sang 'The Man of the West' with much vigour, and when Mr. W. B. Yeats made his appearance he was received with hisses and boohs. The singing of 'A Nation Once Again' was started, and continued until the curtain-raiser was produced. As was the case on the nights previous, 'Riders of the Sea' was well-received.

RECEIVED WITH A HOWL

There was an interval of some 15 minutes before 'The Playboy' was produced. In the meantime the crowd in the stalls was reinforced by a number of young men who, judging from their subsequent applause, were approvers of the play. The vast majority of the audience was, however, decidedly hostile. The first act had scarcely opened when there was a storm of booing and hissing, which drowned the voices of those on the stage for several minutes. The police who, to the number of 30 or more, were lined up on either side of the pit, displayed much activity, but, apparently, they did not discover anybody whose conduct called for removal, and so the 'chucking out' process was not resorted to. There was a howl when the 'Playboy,' Christopher Mahon, appeared, and, after preliminary conversation with 'Pegeen Mike' and her father announced that he was a parricide. The display of hostility was intensified when 'Pegeen,' on the strength of his declaration, showed towards him the most effusive affection. There was some applause, but it was drowned in the expressions of disapproval.

Shortly after the opening of Act II, Mr. Synge, the author, walked out through the stage door and took a seat in the stalls. He was greeted with hisses and some applause. It is in this act [that] Christopher Mahon is greeted with 'a thousand welcomes' because he is the man who killed his father, and when the greeting was extended it was followed by loud booing.

WAS IT INFLUENZA?

At this point a new form of interruption was invented. Everybody in the pit seemed to be attacked by a violent fit of coughing and sneezing, which lasted for a couple of minutes. The supposed parricide was meantime on the stage conversing with 'Pegeen Mike,' but few heard what he said, and when the coughing and sneezing ceased there were cries of 'Lynchehaun!' 'Rotten,' and 'Go in.' The disorder did not continue, however, and the curtain went down on Act II, without any exciting incident taking place.

As soon as the lights were turned on for the interval a young man in the body of the pit began to sing, in stentorian tones, 'The Man of the West,' and the chorus was taken up by many voices. The audience was then

treated to 'The West's Asleep,' and so the time went on until Act III began.

Again there was an outburst of hissing, but this time it was of a mild character, and, a few minutes later, a number of young men walked ostentatiously out from the pit shouting as they went—'Rotten.' It seemed as if there was about to be a disturbance, and the police were again active, while voices from the stalls called out 'No Suppression.'

A CALMER ENDING

In a brief space quiet was again restored, to be broken by a momentary altercation between two gentlemen who occupied seats at the back of the stalls. They separated after exchanging 'courtesies,' and the remainder of the proceedings may be described as tame. It is true that there was much booing when the curtain dropped, but there was also no inconsiderable applause, and the angry passions which were manifested at the conclusion of the previous nights' performances were altogether absent. The theatre was empty in the space of a few minutes without any efforts on the part of the police.

Outside there was a large force of police, while at the junction of Abbey street and O'Connell street another body of men was posted. The crowds which had collected were moved on, and at 11 o'clock the utmost order prevailed.

Early in the night two young men who are alleged to have been creating a disturbance in the theatre were arrested, and taken to Store street Station. They were subsequently released on bail, and will be charged in the Police Court this morning.

MR. SYNGE 'BEAMING'

The author, Mr. J. M. Synge, was beaming at the reception accorded to 'The Playboy' when he was approached by a representative of the 'Independent.' Beyond expressing his gratification at having at last got something like a fair hearing, he had little to say.

Our representative asked him if he thought the use of such 'jaw-breakers' as 'potentate,' 'retribution,' etc., were typical of the conversation of such places as that he had selected for his scene.

Mr. Synge laughingly replied that that was just the very place to hear them.[1] He knew peasants such as he had tried to depict, taking the keenest delight in airing any big words of which they had got hold. As an instance, he said, he heard a poor old woman who was absolutely illiterate say 'I have to use all sorts of stratagems to keep the hens out.'

NOTE

1. In his Preface to *The Playboy of the Western World* Synge declares that all the words and idioms used in his plays have actually been heard by him from the lips of the peasantry. The Anglo-Irish idiom was not discovered, much less invented by Synge—Dr Douglas Hyde and Lady Gregory had used it before him in their renderings of old Irish literature—and in its main peculiarities it is a genuine folk speech in which Gaelic locutions are substituted for current English, and some older English words and usages, gone out of fashion in modern English, are retained; as Yeats put it, it is 'the beautiful English which has grown up in Irish-speaking districts, and takes its vocabulary from the time of Malory and the translators of the Bible, but its idiom and its vivid metaphor from Irish'. Synge, however, writing of a life that, in its external relations, is limited to a little-known locality in a language equally limited, was the first to rise above the essential narrowness implicit in these limitations and construct a drama of universal interest.

An Exciting Experience*

WALTER STARKIE

The most exciting theatrical experience of my youth took place in my thirteenth year when J. M. Synge's Play *The Playboy of the Western World* was produced for the first time at the Abbey Theatre in January 1907. It was my first visit to the Abbey Theatre, and Paddy Tobin, whom at school we all considered an expert in theatrical matters as he had acted with his three cousins, the Wogan Brown girls (all of them excellent actresses, and one of them, Dorothy, so vivacious that she appealed to Bernard Shaw as the ideal embodiment of Dolly in *You Never Can Tell*), promised to bring me round to the Green Room to introduce me to Lady Gregory.

'Tonight,' he said, when I met him at Nelson's Pillar, 'my father says there will be the hell of a row as the newspapers have been publishing attacks on the play, saying that it is an insult to Ireland.' When we reached Abbey Street we found a great crowd assembled in the streets adjoining the theatre. Inside, the atmosphere was electric and there was suspense in the air, as though everyone in the auditorium expected a political revolution to break out. Instead of waiting quietly in their seats for the play to begin, many gathered together in groups talking excitedly, and I was struck, too, by the varying types I saw in the audience. In addition to the usual middle-class theatre-goers, there were numbers of workers, and here and there gentlemen and ladies in evening dress, and young men whose tousled hair and beards proclaimed them initiates of the Dublin Latin quarter. A wizened old man sitting next to me pointed out the literary and political celebrities as they took their places. 'See that long thin rake of a fellow, that's Best[1] the Librarian arguing with Dr R. M. Henry, one of the Belfast

* *Scholars and Gypsies; An Autobiography* (London: John Murray, 1963) pp. 37–9.

Home-Rulers. Next but two to him is a fine upstanding man with a beard: that's AE,[2] our Irish Buddha! Over there by himself is the victim of the evening, John Millington Synge. Every one of the Irish intellectuals are present, but it's not the play they've come to see, but to spy on one another.' I longed to ask the old man for an explanation for his cryptic words, but just then the lights dimmed and I heard a dismal gong sounding the knell as it seemed to me, and the curtain rose.

Although I tried very hard to concentrate upon the play it was impossible to hear the actors after the first few minutes because of the interruptions and disturbances which took place all over the auditorium. When these reached a climax, one[3] of the company advanced to the footlights and tried to appeal for silence. He said, as far as I could make out, that anyone in the audience who did not like the play was at liberty to get up and leave, but nobody left. Instead, pandemonium broke loose, and my wizened neighbour, whom I had considered an inoffensive old man, jumped to his feet shouting: 'Clear the decks! Down with Willie Fay!' And his shouts were taken up in chorus by the gallery. Then came shouts from the pit below and many started to sing the revolutionary song, *The West's asleep*.

While all this rumpus was going on the actors and actresses on the stage continued valiantly to act their parts, but they were puppets; I could see their lips move but hardly a word reached me. Paddy Tobin and I recognized some friends who were from Trinity College. They had come at the request of Lady Gregory's nephew with other students to support the play. Seeing that the disturbances increased in the second act they thought the best way in which they could show their support of the play would be by singing *God Save the King* in chorus. Even today, when I look back at that fateful night in the history of the Irish National Theatre, I cannot imagine how such a crazy notion as singing the British National Anthem could have entered their heads. Instead of pouring oil on troubled waters they enraged the Irish patriots in the pit by singing what the latter considered a political song.

Paddy Tobin and I enjoyed ourselves immensely in the hullabaloo. Through the tempest of shouting and hissing we heard cries '*Sinn Fein Amhain*'[4] and 'kill the author', and from our seats at the side of the gallery we had a wonderful view of the milling mob in the pit and gallery. Then suddenly the doors of the auditorium opened and a posse of Dublin Metropolitan police entered, and many of the rowdy elements were cast out. We expected the burly giants to draw their batons and made ready to join the wild stampede, but there was a momentary lull as another figure advanced to the footlights to speak to the mob; but he was no more successful than his predecessor had been in the first act, and his voice was drowned by catcalls and the strident tones of toy trumpets. Those who thought the display of force by the police would calm the rioters were mistaken, for Act III of the play began amidst scenes of even greater chaos.

As we were unable to hear a single word of the play, and knowing that the fight was spreading to the streets outside, we left our seats and mingled with the crowd in the vestibule. Following Paddy during the interval I managed to reach the back of the stage through a side door leading into the lane, and we joined the actors and their supporters gathered round Lady Gregory and J. M. Synge. While to me it seemed that all the players were wringing their hands, tearing their hair and running hither and thither, Lady Gregory stood at the door of the Green Room as calm and collected as Queen Victoria about to open a charity bazaar. Seeing Paddy Tobin and myself, she beckoned us over and handed each of us a piece of the huge barmbarck which she had baked at Coole and brought up to Dublin for the Abbey cast. While we were munching our cake we observed the author, J. M. Synge, mooning about among the actors like a lost soul. I had seen him on various occasions in Kingstown, and when I passed him striding along the Dalkey road swinging his stick I used to wonder whether he was French or Austrian, for he had moustaches and a little goatee or 'imperial'. When I saw him on the night of the Abbey riot his face was pale and sunken, and he looked like a ghost of the sun-tanned wanderer I had seen walking by the sea. I watched him closely as he sat motionless through the dumb-show of his play, amidst the rioting and insults of the mob, but not a trace of emotion could I discern in his pale mask-like face that gazed unseeing at the raging auditorium.

NOTES

Walter FitzWilliam Starkie (1894–) became a Fellow of Trinity College Dublin in 1920. During the war he was British Council representative in Madrid. He was also a Director of the Abbey Theatre from 1926 to 1942 and a Professor-in-Residence at the University of California at Los Angeles from 1961 to 1967. As a young man he had studied music and played the violin all over Europe, using his skill to acquire friendship of the gipsies and to study their music and folklore. From this came *Raggle Taggle* (1933), an account of his adventures in the Balkans, *Spanish Raggle Taggle* (1934), *Gypsy Folklore & Music* (1935), *The Waveless Plain* (an Italian memoir; 1938), *In Sara's Tents* (1953), *The Road to Santiago* (1957) and *Scholar & Gypsies* (autobiography; 1963)—all reflect this life long interest. In a letter to Lady Gerald Wellesley, dated 30 June 1936, W. B. Yeats described Starkie as a 'fat man . . . who most years spends a couple of months among gypsies in Spain, Austria, etc., playing his fiddle and escaping among the gypsy women, according to one of the reviewers, "a fate worse than death" . . . '

1. Dr Richard Irvine Best (1872–1959), distinguished Gaelic scholar and linguist who was long associated with the National Library of Ireland. A well-known Dublin character and friend of James Joyce and Oliver St John Gogarty, he appears under his own name in *Ulysses* (the National Library episode). Until he arrived in London on 9 January 1903 Synge had met relatively few writers and artists. While he was very much a part of the W. B. Yeats—Lady Gregory circle in Ireland, his only other literary friends were Richard Best and Stephen MacKenna. It was in Paris where Synge first met Best, who had gone there to study Celtic.

2. AE [George Russell] (1867–1935), poet, painter, journalist and social thinker who played a considerable part in the Irish renaissance. He made the *Irish Homestead*, of which he was editor from 1906 to 1923, an important intellectual and literary journal. Although a passionate nationalist, he believed England and Ireland to be economically interdependent and therefore did not join in the Easter Rising of 1916. The most practical of economists and

the most mystical of poets, he was the author of many volumes of essays and poetry. From 1923 to 1930 he was the editor of the *Irish Statesman*. Once, when he was exploring mysticism and theosophy in 1897, Synge went with AE to a meeting of the Theosophical Society. When the first three-year trial period of the Irish Literary Theatre closed and Edward Martyn and George Moore withdrew, Yeats, together with Lady Gregory and AE, in 1902 joined with the Fay brothers and their company.
  3. William G. Fay.
  4. 'Ourselves alone'.

*The Playboy of the Western World**

WILLIAM G. FAY

I wish I could say the same for 1907, the year that proved as stormy in my fortunes as its predecessor had been prosperous, for it began with the historic uproar over *The Playboy of the Western World* and ended with the departure of the Fays from the Abbey Theatre and from Ireland.

I often hear it said that a really great artist is unmoved by the howl of the rabble and goes on producing his work as he pleases, confident that the future will vindicate him. This is true only with some qualification. Great artists have shown magnificent examples of courage in the face of popular hostility, but that is not to say that they have not felt deeply wounded by it, and their resentment is often reflected in their work. A classic case is that of Thomas Hardy, who after *Jude the Obscure* retired from the struggle and devoted the rest of his life to poetry. But not every author, certainly not many young ones, can take the course of dignity and silence. The temptation to hit back is strong, and among those who have yielded to it we find J. M. Synge. He could not forgive the crass ignorance, the fatuity, the malevolence with which *The Well of the Saints* had been received. He had given of his best in good faith, and offence had been taken where no offence had been intended. 'Very well, then,' he said to me bitterly one night, 'the next play I write I will make sure will annoy them.' And he did. As soon as I cast eyes over the script of *The Playboy of the Western World* I knew we were in for serious trouble unless he would consent to alter it drastically. Many and many a time I strove with him, using all the arguments I could muster, to get him to see that if you attack your audience you must expect them to retaliate, that you might as well write to a newspaper and expect the editor not to insist on the last word. The emotions displayed on the stage are designed by the author and interpreted by the players to give the audience

---

* William G. Fay and Catherine Carswell, *The Fays of the Abbey Theatre* (London: Rich and Cowan, 1935) pp. 211–22.

a vicarious experience of them, and if the audience reacts to them, that is the measure of the author's and actors' success. Thus, laughter on the stage makes laughter in the house and anger makes anger. But by laughter I mean straight laughter, not wrath disguised in a grin which the average audience is quick to see through and resent accordingly. Synge could never be made to understand that. He was apt to think in the terms of Zola, who got his effects by keeping all his characters in one key. He could never see that Zola was a novelist, not a dramatist, and that there is all the difference between a printed story that one reads to oneself and the same story told as a play to a mixed audience of varying degrees of intelligence. Frank [1] and I begged him to make Pegeen a decent likeable country girl, which she might easily have been without injury to the play, and to take out the torture scene in the last act where the peasants burn Christy with the lit turf. It was no use referring him to all the approved rules of the theatrical game—that, for example, while a note of comedy was admirable for heightening tragedy, the converse was not true. The things that we wanted him to alter did not amount to five per cent. of the whole play. *The Well of the Saints* had suffered from too much anger. *The Playboy of the Western World* was anger *in excelsis*.[2] The characters were as fine and diverting a set of scallywags as one could invent for one story, but it was years too soon for our audiences to appreciate them as dramatic creations.

Frank and I might as well have saved our breath. We might as well have tried to move the Hill of Howth [3] as move Synge. That was his play, he said, and, barring one or two jots and tittles of 'bad language' that he grudgingly consented to excise, it was the play that with a great screwing up of courage we produced.

I gave the *Playboy* long and careful rehearsal, doing my best to tone down the bitterness of it, and all the time with a sinking heart. I knew we were in for trouble, but it was my business to get Synge's play produced as nearly to his notions as possible in the circumstances and with the material at my disposal. All through the first act the play went splendidly, and I was beginning to feel hopeful, even cheerful. The second act, too, opened to plenty of laughter. We had not got to the beginning of the 'rough stuff.' But with the entrance of the Widow Quin the audience began to show signs of restlessness. Obviously they couldn't abide her; and when we came to my line about 'all bloody fools,' the trouble began in earnest, with hisses and cat-calls and all the other indications that the audience are not in love with you. Now that word 'bloody' in the script had given me qualms, but Synge had insisted—and who was I to contradict him?—that in the West [4] it was the casual mild expletive, like 'bally,' or 'beastly,' or 'bloomin'.' Yet how was Dublin to know that? In Dublin, as for that matter all over England and Scotland in those days, it was a 'low' word, a pothouse word. Quite a lot of years later, even, it provided the theatrical sensation of the London season when Bernard Shaw's Eliza Doolittle rapped it out in *Pygmalion*. Nowadays, I understand, it is so much a young lady's expression that no

he-man ever dreams of using it. Synge was in advance of his time. There was therefore some excuse for the audience's protest, though it was needlessly violent. Yet the queer thing was that what turned the audience into a veritable mob of howling devils was not this vulgar expletive, but as irreproachable a word as there is in the English dictionary—the decent old-fashioned 'shift' for the traditional under-garment of a woman. There is a point in the play where Christy (which in this case was poor me) says, 'It's Pegeen I'm seeking only, and what'd I care if you brought me a drift of chosen females standing in their shifts itself, maybe, from this place to the Eastern World.' You may say that the image—a magnificent one, mark you—must have been shocking to so unsophisticated an audience as ours, but it was not the image that shocked them. It was the word, for the row was just as bad when Pegeen Mike herself said to the Widow Quin, 'Is it you asking for a penn'orth of starch, with ne'er a shift or a shirt as long as you can remember?'

The last act opened with the house in an uproar, and by the time the curtain fell, the uproar had become a riot. Two or three times I tried to get them to let us finish for the sake of those who wanted to hear the play, but it was no use. They wanted a row and they were going to have one. There were free fights in the stalls. Mr. Hillis,[5] our conductor, got his face damaged, and at one time it seemed as if the stage would be stormed. It was lucky for themselves that the patriots did not venture as far as that, for our call-boy, who was also boiler attendant and general factotum, had armed himself with a big axe from the boiler-room, and swore by all the saints in the calendar that he would chop the head off the first lad who came over the footlights. And knowing him, I haven't a shadow of doubt that he would have chopped.

This was on a Saturday night. Over Sunday the directors had to consider whether they would bow to the storm and withdraw the play, or face it out. Very properly they took the courageous course, and the company, though it was no joke for them, loyally supported their decision to go on playing at all costs. And so on the Monday night the curtain was rung up to a well-organised pandemonium, for the patriots had been busy over the week-end also. As it was impossible for any of us to be heard, I arranged with the cast that we should simply walk through the play, not speaking a word aloud, but changing positions and going through all the motions, so to speak. The noise was terrific, but we finished the play. It was not until the Thursday night that, in order to give a fair deal to those who had paid their money to hear, the directors had the police in the theatre. We also had taken the precaution to pad the floor with felt, which frustrated the rhythmic stamping that had been the opposition's most effective device. Thus we were able once more to speak the lines, but our reputation as an Irish national institution was ruined. Not content with libelling the saintly Irish people, we had actually called in the tyrant Saxon's myrmidons to silence their righteous indignation! Of course the

root of the trouble was that Synge had written a brilliant play about the Irish peasantry without any of the traditional sentiment or illusions that were then so dear to the Irish playgoer. He was accused of making a deliberate attack on the national character, whatever that may be. Even William Boyle[6] was among the angriest of angry, though he had to confess that he had not seen the play but had only read the reports of the hubbub in the newspapers. To mark his loathing of us he withdrew all his plays, which I think was ungrateful, considering all we had done for him.

The uproar, of course, was not confined to the theatre. It re-echoed, with terrific amplification, in the Press, and Dublin in those days was peculiarly rich in organs of public opinion which ordinarily made a discordant chorus, but now were enabled to bray all together in something that was almost harmony. One or two writers ventured to 'praise with faint damns,' but damning of some sort was *de rigueur*.[7] Arthur Griffith was particularly venomous, and incidentally managed to make an ass of himself. He declared that 'shift' and 'bloody' were not the worst of Synge's verbal offences, that he and several friends present with him would take their Bible oath that another word, a nauseating word, a cloacine word was used. On being confronted with the script he had to admit (which he did with a very ill grace) that, in his eagerness to hear evil, he had misheard a perfectly innocent and commonplace word that sounds a little like it. Even more discreditable than this flight of imagination was his attack on the Abbey Theatre as an anti-Irish institution financed by English money, which was his agreeable way of describing Miss Horniman's generosity. The strictures of the dramatic critics and the fulminations of the leader-writers were followed up by the hysterics of the correspondence columns. Most of the letters were incredibly funny, though at the time we could not be expected to appreciate their humour. There was, for example, 'A Girl from the West,'[8] from whom I cannot help quoting a sentence:

> Every character uses coarse expressions, and Miss Allgood (one of the most charming actresses I have ever seen) is forced to use a word indicating an essential item of female attire which the lady would probably never utter in ordinary circumstances even to herself.

So you see the difficulties that beset a respectable Irishwoman when she goes into a shop to buy a chemise! It was this sort of nonsense that inspired the following verses in the *Dublin Evening Mail*. I have never definitely ascertained the authorship, but I suspect the late Susan Mitchell, 'Æ's' secretary.

THE BLUSHES OF IRELAND

Oh really, Mr. Yeats (or Yates),
   Oh really really, William Butler,
Your language fairly beats (or bates)
   A Saxon sutler.

You're quite too dense to understand
    The chill—the thrill—of modest loathing
With which one hears on Irish land
    Of underclothing.

Allusions to a flannel shirt
    (Young man, remember this, I urge'ee)
Afflict with agonising hurt
    Our patriot clergy.

And you, sir, you and Mr. Synge,
    In spite of virtue's no-surrender,
You go and make the shameful thing
    Of female gender.

Oppressor! thrust us to the Wall,
    Bid bravo bobbies beat us yellow,
We'll raise an *Independent* bawl,
    A *Freeman's* bellow.

We tell you to your brazen face,
    A score of brogues in concord lifted,
That Ireland never was a place
    Where clothes were sh—fted.

You come, sir, with your English ways,
    Your morals of the Cockney cabby,
Corrupting with unseemly phrase
    The Abbey babby.

Unless we watch your wanton text,
    And waken shame with boos and knockings,
You'll want that poor Miss Allgood next
    To mention st—ck—ngs.

Unless we curb from hour to hour
    This frenzied cult of Aphrodite,
You'll urge reluctant Ambrose Power
    To name his n—ghty.

We'll shriek—we'll faint—we won't be mute
    Until we've forced you to elimi-
nate that vile word, and substitute
    The chaster sh—mmy.

And, look, sir, do not sh—ft your scenes—
    There's scandal aided and abetted.
Let them now virtue intervenes
    Be chemisetted.

Yield Willie! else your day is done,
  Boyles will break out, and health desert you;
The little Fays your doors will shun
  In wounded virtue.

We played *The Playboy* for the full number of advertised performances, matinée included. There was a debate conducted by Mr. Yeats in the theatre on the following Monday, when both sides were given an opportunity of stating their views, but it was a rather futile meeting, I think. The incident was a lamentable business from every point of view, as the future proved. If it taught the public that they could not dictate the policy of the theatre, that was all. However, you cannot beat the public in the end, as I had warned Synge and the other directors, because they can always boycott you. And that was what happened after *The Playboy*. For weeks on end we had to play to five or ten shillings a night—a full programme to half a dozen people scattered all over the house. I used to invite them all into the stalls to sit together. You can play serious plays to a scattered audience, but you cannot play comedy unless somebody laughs, and people do not laugh unless they are sitting together. I lost friends who never forgave me for producing the play and myself taking the leading part, and who could not, or would not understand that it was my job to produce any play that my directors wanted, quite apart from my personal likes or dislikes. All our hard work from the November of the previous year was forgotten—all the previous plays that we had produced to the general delight. Where actors are concerned the public has a very short memory.

One thing that made Synge's plays difficult for a Dublin audience was that he actually knew the people he was writing about, whereas they only thought they did. One could get a fairly accurate and just criticism of a Gaelic play from anyone who spoke the language, for such a person had first-hand knowledge of the peasant. But I don't suppose half a dozen people in Dublin could have told you the difference in idiom and brogue between a man from the glens of Antrim and a man from Waterford, or between a Galway man and a Wicklow one. I myself knew these distinctions in a rough-and-ready way owing to my experience as a stroller and I knew how right Synge was. Time has justified him, for his dialect is now the standard one and is even used by Eugene O'Neill in America. And not only did the Dubliners fail to appreciate Synge's profound knowledge of rural Ireland, but they completely misunderstood the character of the man. He was popularly imagined as an outlandish ogre, actuated by hatred of the human race in general and of the Irish race in particular, and both willing to wound and unafraid to strike. Nothing could have been farther from the truth. Synge would never willingly have hurt anybody. He was one of the gentlest souls that ever breathed, and beloved by everybody who knew him. I never knew him lose his temper even in the most trying circumstances, and he was always full of jokes and good-

humour that made even a long night journey on tour—and that is a severe test for anyone—a pleasure instead of the penance that it usually is. He was a bit of a Quixotic too. I remember, when I was living in High Street, Synge and I one night were walking through one of the roughest of the back streets when we heard the screams of a woman and child coming from behind the shutters of a tumbledown shop and a man's voice shouting and swearing. Synge stopped at once and wanted to go to the rescue. Knowing the quarter I warned him that we should get a rough house if we interfered, but that did not stop him. He began hammering away at the door, the screams getting louder and louder all the time. As he got no reply to his knocking we put our shoulders to the door, and with a combined push smashed it in. It was pitch dark inside but Synge managed to grab the woman while I grabbed the baby, and we got them out. Not content with that we dashed back to the shop and yanked the man out of the house into the street also. He swore powerfully, and was at first inclined to show fight, but a short arm from Synge, planted nicely under his chin, knocked him up against the wall and reduced him to a comparatively reasonable frame of mind. The mother and child were put back into the shop and told to lock the door. Then we walked the man down the street between us, intending to hand him over to the police, but on the way Synge suddenly changed his mind and chased him off instead. After that he resumed the discussion of the first principles of dramatic construction as if nothing had happened. Next day, as I was passing along the same street, I saw the man and his wife sitting on a stool by their door laughing and joking while the infant played at their feet!

NOTES

For a note on William G. Fay see p. 29.
 1. Frank Fay, William G. Fay's brother. For a note on him see p. 29.
 2. In the highest degree.
 3. Howth is a peninsula which forms the northern arm of Dublin Bay and rises to approximately 350 feet.
 4. West of Ireland.
 5. G. R. Hillis became conductor in 1906 and remained with the Abbey Theatre until 1908, when he was replaced by John F. Larchet.
 6. William Boyle (1853–1922), Irish dramatist who was among the first playwrights to write for the Abbey Theatre. His plays include *The Building Fund* (1905), one of his best-known and most successful plays, *The Eloquent Dempsey* (1906) and *The Mineral Workers* (1906). Boyle, resenting *The Playboy of the Western World* as a misrepresentation of the Irish peasantry, withdrew his own plays from the Abbey Theatre repertoire, but W. G. Fay at length persuaded him to give them back. See William Boyle, 'Letter to the Editor', *Freeman's Journal* (Dublin) (4 Feb 1907) p. 4 and W. B. Yeats, 'Mr. Boyle's Plays', *Evening Telegraph* (Dublin) (6 Feb 1907) p. 3.
 7. Indispensable; absolutely required by etiquette.
 8. For a record of the press reviews of the first production of *The Playboy of the Western World* see E. H. Mikhail, *J. M. Synge: A Bibliography of Criticism* (London: Macmillan, 1975) pp. 133–44.

J. M. Synge and the Ireland of his Time*

W. B. YEATS

On Saturday, January 26, 1907, I was lecturing in Aberdeen, and when my lecture was over I was given a telegram which said, 'Play great success.' It had been sent from Dublin after the second act of *The Playboy of the Western World*, then being performed for the first time. After one in the morning, my host brought to my bedroom this second telegram, 'Audience broke up in disorder at the word shift.' I knew no more until I got the Dublin papers on my way from Belfast to Dublin on Tuesday morning. On the Monday night no word of the play had been heard. About forty young men had sat in the front seats of the pit, and stamped and shouted and blown trumpets from the rise to the fall of the curtain. On the Tuesday night also the forty young men were there. They wished to silence what they considered a slander upon Ireland's womanhood. Irish women would never sleep under the same roof with a young man without a chaperon, nor admire a murderer, nor use a word like 'shift'; nor could any one recognise the country men and women of Davis[1] and Kickham[2] in these poetical, violent, grotesque persons, who used the name of God so freely, and spoke of all things that hit their fancy.

A patriotic journalism which had seen in Synge's capricious imagination the enemy of all it would have young men believe, had for years prepared for this hour, by that which is at once the greatest and most ignoble power of journalism, the art of repeating a name again and again with some ridiculous or evil association. The preparation had begun after the first performance of *The Shadow of the Glen,* Synge's first play, with an assertion made in ignorance, but repeated in dishonesty, that he had taken his fable and his characters, not from his own mind nor that profound knowledge of cot and curragh he was admitted to possess, but 'from a writer of the Roman decadence.' Some spontaneous dislike had been but natural, for genius like his can but slowly, amid what it has of harsh and strange, set forth the nobility of its beauty, and the depth of its compassion; but the

---

* Extracted from *Forum* (New York) XLVI (Aug 1911) 179–200, reprinted in *Synge and the Ireland of His Time* (Dundrum, Dublin: Cuala Press, 1911), in *The Cutting of An Agate* (London and New York: Macmillan, 1912) pp. 146–95, in *Essays* (London and New York: Macmillan, 1924) pp. 385–424, and in *Essays and Introductions* (London and New York: Macmillan, 1961) pp. 311–40.

frenzy that would have silenced his master-work was, like most violent things, artificial, that defence of virtue by those who have but little, which is the pomp and gallantry of journalism and its right to govern the world. As I stood there watching, knowing well that I saw the dissolution of a school of patriotism that held sway over my youth, Synge came and stood beside me, and said, 'A young doctor has just told me that he can hardly keep himself from jumping on to a seat, and pointing out in that howling mob those whom he is treating for venereal disease.'

* * *

I attack things that are as dear to many as some holy image carried hither and thither by some broken clan, and can but say that I have felt in my body the affections I disturb, and believed that if I could raise them into contemplation I would make possible a literature that, finding its subject-matter all ready in men's minds, would be, not as ours is, an interest for scholars, but the possession of a people. I have founded societies with this aim, and was indeed founding one in Paris when I first met with J. M. Synge, and I have known what it is to be changed by that I would have changed, till I became argumentative and unmannerly, hating men even in daily life for their opinions. And though I was never convinced that the anatomies of last year's leaves are a living forest, nor thought a continual apologetic could do other than make the soul a vapour and the body a stone, nor believed that literature can be made by anything but by what is still blind and dumb within ourselves, I have had to learn how hard, in one who lives where forms of expression and habits of thought have been born, not for the pleasure of begetting, but for the public good, is that purification from insincerity, vanity, malignity, arrogance, which is the discovery of style. But life became sweet again when I had learnt all I had not learnt in shaping words, in defending Synge against his enemies, and knew that rich energies, fine, turbulent or gracious thoughts, whether in life or letters, are but love-children.

Synge seemed by nature unfitted to think a political thought, and with the exception of one sentence, spoken when I first met him in Paris, that implied some sort of Nationalist conviction, I cannot remember that he spoke of politics or showed any interest in men in the mass, or in any subject that is studied through abstractions and statistics. Often for months together he and I and Lady Gregory would see no one outside the Abbey Theatre, and that life, lived as it were in a ship at sea, suited him, for unlike those whose habit of mind fits them to judge of men in the mass, he was wise in judging individual men, and as wise in dealing with them as the faint energies of ill-health would permit; but of their political thoughts he long understood nothing. One night, when we were still producing plays in a little hall, certain members of the company told him that a play on the Rebellion of '98 would be a great success. After a fortnight he brought

them a scenario which read like a chapter out of Rabelais. Two women, a Protestant and a Catholic, take refuge in a cave, and there quarrel about religion, abusing the Pope or Queen Elizabeth and Henry VIII, but in low voices, for the one fears to be ravished by the soldiers, the other by the rebels. At last one woman goes out because she would sooner any fate than such wicked company. Yet I doubt if he would have written at all if he did not write of Ireland, and for it, and I know that he thought creative art could only come from such preoccupation. Once when, in later years, anxious about the educational effect of our movement, I proposed adding to the Abbey Company a second company to play international drama, Synge, who had not hitherto opposed me, thought the matter so important that he did so in a formal letter.

I had spoken of a German municipal theatre as my model, and he said that the municipal theatres all over Europe gave fine performances of old classics, but did not create (he disliked modern drama for its sterility of speech, and perhaps ignored it), and that we would create nothing if we did not give all our thoughts to Ireland. Yet in Ireland he loved only what was wild in its people, and in 'the grey and wintry sides of many glens.' All the rest, all that one reasoned over, fought for, read of in leading articles, all that came from education, all that came down from Young Ireland—though for this he had not lacked a little sympathy—first wakened in him perhaps that irony which runs through all he wrote; but once awakened, he made it turn its face upon the whole of life. The women quarrelling in the cave would not have amused him if something in his nature had not looked out on most disputes, even those wherein he himself took sides, with a mischievous wisdom. He told me once that when he lived in some peasant's house, he tried to make those about him forget that he was there, and it is certain that he was silent in any crowded room. It is possible that low vitality helped him to be observant and contemplative, and made him dislike, even in solitude, those thoughts which unite us to others, much as we all dislike, when fatigue or illness has sharpened the nerves, hoardings covered with advertisements, the fronts of big theatres, big London hotels, and all architecture which has been made to impress the crowd. What blindness did for Homer, lameness for Hephaestus,[3] asceticism for any saint you will, bad health did for him by making him ask no more of life than that it should keep him living, and above all perhaps by concentrating his imagination upon one thought, health itself. I think that all noble things are the result of warfare; great nations and classes, of warfare in the visible world, great poetry and philosophy, of invisible warfare, the division of a mind within itself, a victory, the sacrifice of a man to himself. I am certain that my friend's noble art, so full of passion and heroic beauty, is the victory of a man who in poverty and sickness created from the delight of expression, and in the contemplation that is born of the minute and delicate arrangement of images, happiness and health of mind. Some early poems have a morbid melancholy, and he himself spoke of

early work he had destroyed as morbid, for as yet the craftsmanship was not fine enough to bring the artist's joy which is of one substance with that of sanctity. In one poem he waits at some street-corner for a friend, a woman perhaps, and while he waits and gradually understands that nobody is coming, he sees two funerals and shivers at the future; and in another, written on his twenty-fifth birthday, he wonders if the twenty-five years to come shall be as evil as those gone by. Later on, he can see himself as but a part of the spectacle of the world and mix into all he sees that flavour of extravagance, or of humour, or of philosophy, that makes one understand that he contemplates even his own death as if it were another's and finds in his own destiny but, as it were, a projection through a burning-glass of that general to men. There is in the creative joy an acceptance of what life brings, because we have understood the beauty of what it brings, or a hatred of death for what it takes away, which arouses within us, through some sympathy perhaps with all other men, an energy so noble, so powerful, that we laugh aloud and mock, in the terror or the sweetness of our exaltation, at death and oblivion.

*   *   *

'When I got up this morning,' he writes, after he had been a long time in Inishmaan,[4] 'I found that the people had gone to Mass and latched the kitchen door from the outside, so that I could not open it to give myself light.

'I sat for nearly an hour beside the fire with a curious feeling that I should be quite alone in this little cottage. I am so used to sitting here with the people that I have never felt the room before as a place where any man might live and work by himself. After a while as I waited, with just light enough from the chimney to let me see the rafters and the greyness of the walls, I became indescribably mournful, for I felt that this little corner on the face of the world, and the people who live in it, have a peace and dignity from which we are shut for ever.'

This life, which he describes elsewhere as the most primitive left in Europe, satisfied some necessity of his nature. Before I met him in Paris he had wandered over much of Europe, listening to stories in the Black Forest, making friends with servants and with poor people, and this from an aesthetic interest, for he had gathered no statistics, had no money to give, and cared nothing for the wrongs of the poor, being content to pay for the pleasure of eye and ear with a tune upon the fiddle. He did not love them the better because they were poor and miserable, and it was only when he found Inishmaan and the Blaskets, where there is neither riches nor poverty, neither what he calls 'the nullity of the rich' nor 'the squalor of the poor,' that his writing lost its old morbid brooding, that he found his genius and his peace. Here were men and women who under the weight of their necessity lived, as the artist lives, in the presence of death and childhood,

and the great affections and the orgiastic moment when life outleaps its limits, and who, as it is always with those who have refused or escaped the trivial and the temporary, had dignity and good manners where manners mattered. Here above all was silence from all our great orator took delight in, from formidable men, from moral indignation, from the 'sciolist' who 'is never sad,' from all in modern life that would destroy the arts; and here, to take a thought from another playwright of our school, he could love time as only women and great artists do and need never sell it.

*   *   *

As I read *The Aran Islands* right through for the first time since he showed it me in manuscript, I come to understand how much knowledge of the real life of Ireland went to the creation of a world which is yet as fantastic as the Spain of Cervantes. Here is the story of *The Playboy*, of *The Shadow of the Glen;* here is the ghost on horseback and the finding of the young man's body of *Riders to the Sea*, numberless ways of speech and vehement pictures that had seemed to owe nothing to observation, and all to some overflowing of himself, or to some mere necessity of dramatic construction. I had thought the violent quarrels of *The Well of the Saints* came from his love of bitter condiments, but here is a couple that quarrel all day long amid neighbours who gather as for a play. I had defended the burning of Christy Mahon's leg on the ground that an artist need but make his characters self-consistent, and yet that too was observation, for 'although these people are kindly towards each other and their children, they have no sympathy for the suffering of animals, and little sympathy for pain when the person who feels it is not in danger.' I had thought it was in the wantonness of fancy Martin Doul accused the smith of plucking his living ducks, but a few lines farther on, in this book where moral indignation is unknown, I read, 'Sometimes when I go into a cottage, I find all the women of the place down on their knees plucking the feathers from live ducks and geese.'

He loves all that has edge, all that is salt in the mouth, all that is rough to the hand, all that heightens the emotions by contest, all that stings into life the sense of tragedy; and in this book, unlike the plays where nearness to his audience moves him to mischief, he shows it without thought of other taste than his. It is so constant, it is all set out so simply, so naturally, that it suggests a correspondence between a lasting mood of the soul and this life that shares the harshness of rocks and wind. The food of the spiritual-minded is sweet, an Indian scripture says, but passionate minds love bitter food. Yet he is no indifferent observer, but is certainly kind and sympathetic to all about him. When an old and ailing man, dreading the coming winter, cries at his leaving, not thinking to see him again, and he notices that the old man's mitten has a hole in it where the palm is accustomed to the stick, one knows that it is with eyes full of interested

affection as befits a simple man and not in the curiosity of study. When he had left the Blaskets for the last time, he travelled with a lame pensioner who had drifted there, why Heaven knows, and one morning have missed him from the inn where they were staying, he believed he had gone back to the island, and searched everywhere and questioned everybody, till he understood of a sudden that he was jealous as though the island were a woman.

The book seems dull if you read much at a time, as the later Kerry essays[5] do not, but nothing that he has written recalls so completely to my senses the man as he was in daily life; and as I read, there are moments when every line of his face, every inflection of his voice, grows so clear in memory that I cannot realise that he is dead. He was no nearer when we walked and talked than now while I read these unarranged, unspeculating pages, wherein the only life he loved with his whole heart reflects itself as in the still water of a pool. Thought comes to him slowly, and only after long seemingly unmeditative watching, and when it comes (and he had the same character in matters of business), it is spoken without hesitation and never changed. His conversation was not an experimental thing, an instrument of research, and this made him silent; while his essays recall events, on which one feels that he pronounces no judgment even in the depth of his own mind, because the labour of Life itself had not yet brought the philosophic generalisation which was almost as much his object as the emotional generalisation of beauty. A mind that generalises rapidly, continually prevents the experience that would have made it feel and see deeply, just as a man whose character is too complete in youth seldom grows into any energy of moral beauty. Synge had indeed no obvious ideals, as these are understood by young men, and even, as I think, disliked them, for he once complained to me that our modern poetry was but the poetry 'of the lyrical boy,' and this lack makes his art have a strange wildness and coldness, as of a man born in some far-off spacious land and time.

* * *

There are artists like Byron, like Goethe, like Shelley, who have impressive personalities, active wills and all their faculties at the service of the will; but he belonged to those who, like Wordsworth, like Coleridge, like Goldsmith, like Keats, have little personality, so far as the casual eye can see, little personal will, but fiery and brooding imagination. I cannot imagine him anxious to impress or convince in any company, or saying more than was sufficient to keep the talk circling. Such men have the advantage that all they write is a part of knowledge, but they are powerless before events and have often but one visible strength, the strength to reject from life and thought all that would mar their work, or deafen them in the doing of it; and only this so long as it is a passive act. If Synge had married

young or taken some profession, I doubt if he would have written books or been greatly interested in a movement like ours; but he refused various opportunities of making money in what must have been an almost unconscious preparation. He had no life outside his imagination, little interest in anything that was not its chosen subject. He hardly seemed aware of the existence of other writers. I never knew if he cared for work of mine, and do not remember that I had from him even a conventional compliment, and yet he had the most perfect modesty and simplicity in daily intercourse, self-assertion was impossible to him. On the other hand, he was useless amidst sudden events. He was much shaken by the *Playboy* riot; on the first night confused and excited, knowing not what to do, and ill before many days, but it made no difference in his work. He neither exaggerated out of defiance nor softened out of timidity. He wrote on as if nothing had happened, altering *The Tinker's Wedding* to a more unpopular form, but writing a beautiful serene *Deirdre*, with, for the first time since his *Riders to the Sea*, no touch of sarcasm or defiance. Misfortune shook his physical nature while it left his intellect and his moral nature untroubled. The external self, the mask, the *persona*, was a shadow; character was all.

* * *

I remember saying once to Synge that though it seemed to me that a conventional descriptive passage encumbered the action at the moment of crisis, I liked *The Shadow of the Glen* better than *Riders to the Sea*, that seemed for all the nobility of its end, its mood of Greek tragedy, too passive in suffering, and had quoted from Matthew Arnold's introduction to *Empedocles on Etna* to prove my point. Synge answered: 'It is a curious thing that *Riders to the Sea* succeeds with an English but not with an Irish audience, and *The shadow of the Glen*, which is not liked by an English audience, is always liked in Ireland, though it is disliked there in theory.'

NOTES

In 1905 C. P. Scott of the *Manchester Guardian* commissioned Synge to do a series of articles on those impoverished areas of the west of Ireland known as the Congested Districts. Synge was accompanied by the painter Jack B. Yeats, who was to do the sketches. Scott was enthusiastic about the articles. 'You have done capitally for us, and with Mr. Yeats have helped to bring home to people here the life of those remote districts as it can hardly have been done before.' A Dublin publisher named Whaley wanted to reprint the articles in book form, but Synge refused, feeling perhaps that they were not finished enough. W. B. Yeats apparently either felt the same way about them or knew of Synge's reservations because he refused to allow them to be included in the posthumous Collected Edition of Synge's works. When George Roberts, manager of Maunsel and Company which published the edition, insisted on their being included and was supported by Synge's brother Edward, who found a note in Synge's hand among his papers apparently sanctioning it, Yeats withdrew his co-operation and published separately the introduction he had written for the edition under the title 'Synge and the Ireland of His Time'.

1. Thomas Osborne Davis (1814–45), Irish writer and politician who was the chief organiser and poet of the Young Ireland movement. He wrote patriotic verses such as 'A

Nation Once Again' and 'The Battle of Fontenoy'. His writings virtually became the gospel of the Sinn Fein movement. His *Essays and Poems, with a Centenary Memoir, 1845–1945* appeared in 1945.

  2. Charles Joseph Kickham (1826–82), Irish poet and novelist whose nationalistic writings were immensely popular in Ireland throughout the nineteenth century. *Knocknagow* (1879) is generally accepted as his finest work.

  3. Greek god of fire, with whom the Romans subsequently identified Vulcanus. Charis is the wife of Hephaestus in the *Iliad*; Aphrodite in the *Odyssey*.

  4. One of the Aran Islands.

  5. *In West Kerry*, first published in three successive numbers, Summer, Autumn and Winter 1907, of the *Shanachie*.

My Memories of John Synge[*]

PADRAIC COLUM

At twenty-six John Synge, according to 'C. H. H.,'[1] 'was a strongly-built man with a rather thick neck and large head, a wonderful face with great luminous sad eyes, and though he was tanned from being constantly out of doors, there was a sort of pallor on his face that gave it a look of delicacy belying his figure, which was that of a hardy mountaineer.' I first met him when he was seven years older. His face was grey; he had kindly hazel eyes, and he wore with his moustache a little chin-tuft; his brow went up steeply, and he had strong hair that was neither black nor brown. In a way he was like Fritz Kreisler[2]—less couth, less vivacious, wearing rougher clothes, but still as like as a brother might be who had gone, not on to the platform, but into the study. He was a walker, a man with a deliberate pace, who, out of doors, invariably carried a stick in his hand. In a room he was a listener; he kept neither aloof nor apart, but in a city of people who talked eagerly, he, with that strongly modelled head of his held so well up and with his air as of a foreign student, was noticeably quiet and unassuming. He was not like any poet I have known, and I think he must have been like some of the European musicians; when 'C. H. H.' visited his people in Wicklow he had just come back from Germany where he had been studying music; with the fiddle that he carried about with him he was able to make himself companionable by many a hearth-fire in peasant Ireland.—

> Four strings I've brought from Spain and France
> To make your long men skip and prance,
> Till stars come out to watch the dance,
> Where nets are laid to dry.

The stick that he carried had a history; it was, if I remember aright, of some

[*] *The Road Round Ireland* (New York: Macmillan, 1926) pp. 357–70.

heavy African wood; it had been presented by one of the Boer generals to John MacBride of the Boer – Irish Brigade. From him it had come to Stephen MacKenna—not Stephen MacKenna [*sic*] the novelist. Synge had borrowed the stick, and by no persuasion could his friend Stephen MacKenna get it back from him. On many a lonely tramp it was with him, and he died with the stick unalienated from him. Once, with that stick in his hands, he had stood against a charge of police in a street in Dublin. But the crowd that had drawn the police fled, and then John Synge turned away, resolved, as a friend of his told me, not to take seriously again any physical-force demonstration in Ireland.

There was nothing about Synge to make a crowd throw up a hat for; he was a made man in a city of men in the making; he could not have been a popular figure in Dublin. But his work might have been presented in such a way that it would have been tolerated from the beginning and that it would have been respected before his own end. And this would have happened, I believe, if the entrance for him had not been made somewhat intimidatingly. 'A play that is like one of Aeschylus's' William Butler Yeats announced when he had read 'Riders to the Sea.' 'Who is Aeschylus? Oh, he's the man who writes like John Synge.' In that characteristic way Dublin countered the claim that Yeats set up.

The Opposition to His First Plays

On the eve of the production of his first play 'The Shadow of the Glen,' the tendencies of Synge's work were made highly controversial in a controversial city. John Butler Yeats, with the best intentions in the world, wrote an article[3] in Arthur Griffith's paper 'The United Irishman,' praising the new play for being a satire on peasant marriages in Ireland. The new dramatist was going to show a young woman leaving her house and husband to go with a tramp upon the roads. And the production of his play would signal the end of the sort of marriage, too common in peasant Ireland, where property and not love was the consideration. The article was read by the sort of man and woman who were ready to fight for their ideal of Ireland—and their ideal did not include a country in which such happenings were celebrated. The readers of John Butler Yeats' article got the notion that Synge was a propagandist for certain alien ideas.

In the Ireland of the time, an Ireland that was still being defamed by the Unionist press and by innumerable Unionist institutions, there was a very ready defence-mechanism. Who was John Synge? He was Anglo-Irish—that was certain; he was of the land-owning class, the class that raked all that muck about Ireland into English journals and into religio-politico-publications. As a matter of fact John Synge's family had a very good record in Irish affairs. Says 'C. H. H.', 'He told me he was immensely proud that his grandfather was one of the "Twelve Righteous Men," having refused a peerage at the time of the Union.' However, the defence-mechanism was set up for the production of 'The Shadow of the Glen.' The

virtue of her women was what distinguished Ireland from the decivilised lands to the east of her!

And so a hostile sentiment was in existence before the first production of a Synge play. I believe that if 'Riders to the Sea' had been given first—and it came into the hands of the directors at the same time as 'The Shadow of the Glen'—Synge would have started under less unfavourable auspices. But this would not have mattered very much, I suppose; he would have had to fight the hundred-per-cent Irelanders.

His First Production

The first production of 'The Shadow of the Glen' was in 1903, in the Molesworth Hall. This hall that is in a quiet street has some connection with a Protestant Church. Mrs. Hemans[4] is buried in the little cemetery back of it. There the hardly-fledged National Theatre Society gave its plays on Thursdays, Fridays, and Saturdays, with new productions every month in the season. Before this I had become acquainted with Synge. I had met him when he was being introduced to the members of the Society, and I had seen him at rehearsals in the Camden Street Hall—rehearsals of his own play and of 'The King's Threshold.' I was standing with him at the back of the hall on the night of the first production of 'The Shadow of the Glen.' The hall is quite a small one; it holds, perhaps, three hundred people; the stage is just a platform, and there is a small gallery at the back of the hall. We stood together under the gallery, with our backs to the door by which the audience entered.

When the curtain fell on 'The Shadow of the Glen' it was plain that the audience was disconcerted. There was applause from the supporters of the theatre, and there were calls, 'Author, Author!' And then there was a hiss to answer the calls. A woman hissed conscientiously. Synge was shaking. 'Author, author,' came the call. He walked up through the middle of the little hall, mounted the stage and bowed in response to the call. His nervousness was real and constitutional, and this had been an ordeal for him.

At that time, when he was not away in the West of Ireland, he was living in Kingstown with his people, who, I think, had come to live there from the County Wicklow. Kingstown! Above the harbour are genteel houses and 'squares,' and 'parks,' and 'terraces,' with English or Italianised names, and all with faint associations with Victoria and Albert. Land-owners who have no longer any connection with the property they once drew incomes from, retired army and naval officers, retired civil-servants, live in those 'squares' and 'parks' and 'terraces.' I have a vague recollection of seeing Synge in Kingstown a first and second time. The vague part of the recollection is that of seeing him in a detached house on the road to beautiful Killiney. The other part of the recollection is well-kept: I went to see him in a lifeless square called Crossthwait [*sic*] Park[5]—one wondered who could have thought of building these big houses in that part of the

world. I went there to talk with him about some plays, for at that time he was on the Reading Committee of the Theatre.

He was ill and in bed, but there was nothing frail or hectic about him. He had been reading medieval French plays; the volume he was engaged on was the only book in the room. I never saw Synge amongst books. Stephen MacKenna, who was his great friend in Paris, told me of the little shelf of books that was across Synge's mantle-shelf there; they were always the same books, and there were never more than a dozen of them—Baudelaire, Villon, Ronsard, I think he named.

On Being with Synge

Then I came to know John Synge quite well. He came to live in a real Dublin suburb—in Rathmines. He had a couple of rooms in the usual rooming-house, and, as I lived near, I would call some afternoons and go for a walk with him. 'The Well of the Saints,' his first three-act play, had been produced; Synge had been in London for the production of his plays by the Irish Theatre there; his reputation was established, and, as a slight fruit of that, he had got some reviewing to do. And so he was there in Rathmines, with his typewriter in action, and a few books from 'The Academy' upon his table.

He worked very slowly on these reviews; it was amusing to see him do intensive work on an elementary book written in Irish either as a text or as a piece of Gaelic League propaganda. He had an income of fifty pounds a year, and the guinea, or half guinea he got for reviewing such books meant something to him. Once or twice a week I would call after lunch, and he and I would go for a walk together. We used to go towards the Dublin hills generally. Synge liked to get away from his work; when you got out on the hills, he said, you realized how exaggerated your feelings were about it. He had a laugh that was half grim, half good-humoured. I remember that laugh of his when he talked of a certain Irish writer who had written all sorts of things. He had just published a book on biology, history, and art. 'When one fails at everything else one writes a book on everything,' Synge said.

He had not really read Yeats' poetry—the volumes were too expensive, but he talked of buying one of them. On one of our walks, I remember, he spoke of a lyric Yeats had read at a gathering the night before—it was one of the choruses out of 'Deirdre.'—

> 'Why is it,' Queen Edain said,
> 'If I do but climb the stair
> To the tower overhead,
> When the winds are calling there,
> Or the gannets calling out,
> In waste places of the sky,
> There's so much to think about,
> That I cry, that I cry?'

But her goodman answered her:
'Love would be a thing of nought
Had not all his limbs a stir
Born out of immoderate thought;
Were he anything by half,
Were his measure running dry.
Lovers, if they may not laugh,
Have to cry, have to cry.'

Synge praised this lyric, saying that it had speech, such speech as is in Blake's poetry, speech that had the directness of life.

Once I spoke to him of the gorgeousness of the dialogue in his own plays. 'Ah,' he said, 'but if you were to see it when it comes out first; it's just bald!' That words became worn out was one of his theories. 'A.E.' disputed this. Words, 'A.E.' maintained, cannot really be made debased; any word used with vision or emotion becomes worthy. 'Awfully he rose before him.' The word 'awfully' had been made the cheapest of words—'It is awfully good of you'—but one who felt the vision or the emotion could use it to describe a divine apparition. Synge, in reply, used to say that words had a cycle of life; the time came when they were too worn out for journalism even; then one might bring them back into dramatic speech again; he had taken up many words that were at the end of their cycle.

These walks gave me a glimpse now and then of the life he had lived when he was young here and when he was in Europe. The birds built their nests in the quiet just before dawn: so he told me once as we walked along the little stream of the Dodder,[6] and I could see him there as a boy, watching the birds build in that quiet time. Then, speaking of Irish traditional singing, he noted how like it was to the singing of the Albanians; he had heard these people sing on the Paris-Constantinople train. He did not tell me of any journey to the East; he only spoke of standing with a crowd in a third-class compartment on the Constantinople train.

All his work was subjective, he once told me, it all came out of moods in his own life. 'Riders to the Sea' had come out of the feeling that old age was coming upon him—he was not forty at the time—and that death was making approach. And it is this sombre personal feeling that makes the play; it is odd to recall now that in Dublin quite intelligent people spoke of it as being reminiscent of Pierre Loti's[7] 'Iceland Fisherman.' James Joyce has told me that he had talked with Synge in Paris about this play: the criticism that Joyce had made of it was that it was too brief to sustain the tragic mood—'You cannot have a tragedy in a play that lasts for twenty minutes.' I think Joyce was mistaken in this view of 'Riders to the Sea': the chanting of the *caoine*[8] for the dead by the kneeling women brings in another temporality to the play; it adds to it, not minutes, but measurements of tragic experience.

He spoke of personal work of another kind that he had done: before

Yeats had found him and had sent him back to Ireland to make himself a playwright he had written something in the form of a diary—the diary of a musician who is so highly strung that he always broke down when he had to face an audience. I thought of Synge's own whitened face and shaking arm when he had appeared at a first production. This diary might have been autobiographical; there was a vague love-story running through it. He never spoke of personal relationships with women nor of love-affairs. A friend of his had told me of Synge's shock on coming before a nude at an exhibition—a gathered-up figure painted in greenish tints, an impressionist picture, I suppose. Synge's simple-minded recoil showed that this was an unfamiliar experience. And I remember that when we talked about a certain Irish writer who was then making public his Parisian experiences, Synge spoke of him with that laugh of his that was half grim, half good-humoured—or rather he spoke of the side of him that paraded these experiences in a grimly humorous way; he had seen the writer in Paris with expensive favourites, and his attitude was that it was all very well for people who had nothing else to do. I have three detached reminiscences of Synge that I shall put in here: one is that he had thought of writing a novel, and that he had an idea about the form he should give it—his idea was that a man writing a novel to-day, instead of letting himself be influenced by the moderns, should go back to the very beginnings of the novel and start from there; I think he mentioned Defoe as the writer whom he had thought of going back to. The other reminiscence is of his once telling me that he was related to Lafcadio Hearn [9]—he spoke of Hearn as being a distant cousin of his. He once talked to me about a medieval French farce that had suggested the plot of 'The Well of the Saints' to him.[10] In the farce two beggars accidently run into the relics of a saint, and are cured of their blindness. They are disgusted, for the cure leads to the loss of their livelihood. I forget how the French farce ended.

'The Playboy of the Western World'

One winter day I remember walking across Phœnix Park with him, and his telling me about a new play that he was planning. It would be an extravagant comedy, and it would turn upon a story that he had heard—the story of a man accused of killing his father and who is given refuge in a West of Ireland village. The psychological action would lie in the rise to self-esteem of a sheepish young man through the dread fascination that is given him by the story of his deed. Synge did not yet know what was to happen in the play: he had planned a scene in the first act—the young man, eating a raw turnip, sidles up to the counter of a public-house to get a glass of porter with the only penny he has—that was to be the opening scene.

He was ill at the time of the first production. I remember well how the play nearly got past the dubiousness of that first-night audience. The third act was near its close when the line that drew the first hiss was spoken—'A

drift of the finest women in the County Mayo standing in their shifts around me.' That hiss was a signal for a riot in the Theatre. They had been disconcerted and impatient before this, but the audience, I think, would not have made any interruption if this line had not been spoken. Still, they had been growing hostile to the play from the point where Christy's father enters. That scene was too representational. There stood a man with horribly-bloodied bandage upon his head, making a figure that took the whole thing out of the atmosphere of high comedy. Originally that excellent actor, W. G. Fay, was in the part of the Playboy. He made the role a little sardonic, and this, too, took from the extravagance of the comedy. Afterwards the Playboy's father was made a less bloody object, and the part of the Playboy in the hands of another actor was given more charm and gaiety, and there was no trouble with the audience. An incident was smoothed out, some lines were dropped. The truth of the matter is that 'The Playboy of the Western World' was written at times when Synge was really ill, and for all its sanity and healthfulness, there are—or rather there were in the first production—lines and an incident that reflected the violence of the sick man. To-day, as it is played, it is one of the popular plays in the Abbey Theatre's repertoire. 'The Playboy of the Western World' dramatises what is most characteristic in Gaelic life—the Gaelic delight in vivid personality.

Last Glimpses of Synge

I do not remember seeing John Synge for a long time after the production of 'The Playboy of the Western World.' He was living in Kingstown once more with his people, and he was having very bad spells of illness. I have a vivid memory of the occasion when I saw him for the last time. I met him in a street in Dublin. He was going out to Kingstown, and I walked with him to Westland Row Station and sat with him for a while on the platform. He had been in hospital: his face was hollow, and although he spoke quietly there was great intensity in his speech. He was working on 'Deirdre of the Sorrows,' and he had, in spite of his illness, got down to the third act. He began to tell me about this act: there would be an open grave on the stage. I spoke doubtfully of the impression that this would make—would it not be a too obvious heightening of the tragic feeling? But he said that he had been close to death, and that the grave was a reality to him, and it was the reality in the tragedy he was writing. I knew how near he had been to death when he spoke to me in that way, but it seemed that now he was in the way of getting well.

And then we heard that Synge was in a private hospital, and that he was not getting well. And then one day, outside of Trinity College, I met W. B. Yeats; he was in a state of exaltation, like one who has seen something very grave and very revealing. 'Synge is dead,' he said to me. I met Padraic Pearse[11] a few streets further on: he was walking gravely with his head bent, thinking, I suppose, of his school and the problem of its finances. I

told him that Synge was dead. 'It's too bad,' he said, and he was silent for a while.

NOTES

Pádraic Colum (1881–1972), Irish poet and playwright who became one of the group of writers, including W. B. Yeats, George Russell, J. M. Synge and Lady Gregory, who are identified with the Irish Literary Renaissance. His play *The Land* (1905) was the Irish Theatre's first success; others were *The Fiddler's House* (1907), *Thomas Muskerry* (1910), *The Desert* (1912) and *Balloon* (1929).

1. See previous memoir—C. H. H., 'John Synge as I Knew Him', p. 3.
2. Fritz Kreisler (1875–1962), violinist, one of the most successful virtuosos of his time and a 'secret' composer of short violin pieces.
3. John B. Yeats, 'Ireland Out of the Dock', *United Irishman* (Dublin) (10 Oct 1903) p. 2.
4. Felicia Dorothea Hemans (1793–1835), English poetess best known for lyrics including *Casabianca, The Better Land, The Treasures of the Deep, The Homes of England*.
5. 31 Crosthwaite Park, Kingston (now Dun Laoghaire).
6. River rising in Dublin Mountains, flowing into Liffey in Dublin. The bank of the Dodder and the grounds of Rathfarnham Castle were Synge's playgrounds in childhood and were the places where he first became interested in natural history. See Edward Stephens, *My Uncle John*, op. cit., pp. 22–3.
7. Pierre Loti (1850–1923), French novelist whose exoticism made him popular in his time and whose themes anticipated some of the central preoccupations of French literature between the world wars. Synge thought Loti the greatest living writer of prose, and he used to say that he wished to do for the peasantry of Western Ireland what Loti had done for the Breton fisherfolk. One of the sources of *Riders to the Sea* is Loti's *Pêcheur d'Islande*, which Synge read for the first time in 1898 just before he went to the Aran Islands. See Maurice Bourgeois, 'Synge and Loti', *Westminster Review* (London) CLXXIX (May 1913) 532–6 and E. H. Mikhail, 'French Influences on Synge', *Revue de littérature comparée* (Paris) XLII (July–Sep 1968) 429–31.
8. The half-savage, half-musical melopeoia known as the keen.
9. Lafcadio Hearn (1850–1904), writer, translator and teacher who in the late nineteenth century introduced through his numerous articles and books the culture and literature of Japan to the West.
10. In the spring of 1895 and the winter of 1896–7 Synge attended courses given at the Sorbonne by Professor Petit de Julleville, the author of *Histoire du Théâtre en France au Moyen-âge*. On 3 October 1903 he made notes of portions of chapters II and III of the volume *La Comédie et les Mœurs au Moyen-âge* (1886). These chapters include a description of Andrieu de la Vigne's *Moralité de l'Aveugle et du Boiteux* (1456). It is clear that this is the 'early French farce' which Synge told Colum that *The Well of the Saints* had been inspired by.
11. Padraic Pearse (1879–1916), leader of Irish nationalism, poet and educator, the first President of the provisional government of the Irish Republic proclaimed in Dublin on Easter Monday, 24 April 1916, and Commander-in-Chief of the Irish forces in the anti-British rising that began on the same day. He was executed by the British forces on 3 May 1916.

Synge in Hospital*

JOSEPH HOLLOWAY

Tuesday, July 6. Miss Kitty Clinch, on looking over a copy of *The Sphere* for last week, came across a likeness of J. M. Synge, and it set her speaking of his life in Elpis just before his death. Poor fellow, he kept murmuring, 'God have mercy on me, God forgive me,' in his delirium just before death. His favourite nurse was a Catholic and used to make him say his prayers each morning and night. She used to pray for him, and he thanked God he had someone to pray for such a sinner. He called her his 'tidy' nurse because she was always in apple pie order when attending on him. He liked her, and she liked him and did everything she could to make his last hours happy. Before he lost consciousness, she sprinkled holy water over him, and he opened his eyes and asked was she baptising him, and then added, 'Perhaps it is best so.'

Not being sure of Heaven, he used to say he'd like to remain as long as he could on earth. The day before he died, he longed to be changed to another room where the sun could shine in and got his wish. He entered his new room saying, 'Now I will see the sun shine,' but, alas, he never did, for he died that night. He was told by Sir Robert Ball the Sunday before he died, that he would not recover, and he begged of the doctor to do something for him like he did before, but the doctor only shook his head in answer to his piteous appeal. He suffered great pain and used to walk up and down the corridor outside his room to get a little relief. Mrs. Huxley, the matron, used to have long chats with him each day; he invariably was writing when she went in, and she would say, 'There you are, tiring yourself again,' and he would say, 'Stay and talk with me, and I won't write any more.'

The nurse who attended him all through his illness thought him the best and gentlest of creatures. Sometimes he was full of fun and called Dr. Parson's attention to her, and said he never heard the doctor praise her for her tidiness (this was said in the spirit of mischief to tease her).

His people used to call to enquire, but never went up to see him. Every day he used to ask were any of his *affectionate* relatives there that day.

It was a terribly sad sight to see Miss O'Neill[1] (to whom he was engaged) enter the room in the morning at eight and find him whom she loved dead.

* *Joseph Holloway's Abbey Theatre; A Selection from His Unpublished Journal 'Impressions of a Dublin Playgoer'*, ed. Robert Hogan and Michael J. O'Neill (Carbondale and Edwardsville, Illinois: Southern Illinois University Press; London and Amsterdam: Feffer and Simons, 1967) pp. 127–9.

When he was dead, his relatives removed him to their home from which his funeral went—though in life they cared not to see him, poor fellow. . . .He read a portion of the Bible each day, but did not care to see minister or priest. Mrs. Huxley actually sent for a minister some days before his death, and he came, and Synge chatted with him about the weather and such-like topics. In his chats with Mrs. Huxley, he often spoke on Woman's Suffrage and such up-to-date matters. Nurse was of opinion that he had much more religion than many who pretended far more. He was very contrite and docile in his last hours. May God have heard his prayers. At times during his illness he was in great good spirits and would chat on for hours at a time. He was greatly liked by all in the Elpis.

NOTE

In 1904 Miss A. E. Horniman, a benevolent Englishwoman, allowed the Irish National Theatre Society an annual subsidy and undertook at her own expense the renovation of the old theatre of the Mechanics' Institute in Abbey Street, Dublin, and lent it rent free for six years to the Society. The entire restoration and decoration of the 'Abbey Theatre' was the work of Irish hands. The architect was Joseph Holloway, C.E., of Dublin. Holloway was a steady supporter of the company and for many years he kept a diary in which he recorded not only his reactions to the plays but also his descriptions of Dublin's leading figures. 'Impressions of a Dublin Playgoer', which runs to some 25 million words jotted down hastily on more than 100,000 pages, is in the National Library of Ireland and for years has been consulted by scholars. See Joseph Holloway, 'John Millington Synge as Critic of Boucicaultian Irish Drama', *Evening Herald* (Dublin) (10 July 1913) p. 2.

1. For a note on 'Maire O'Neill' [Molly Allgood] see p. 73.

Synge and the Early Days of the Abbey*

SEAN O'MAHONY RAHILLY

Maire O'Neill, she for whom John Millington Synge wrote specially his greatest plays, 'The Playboy of the Western World' and 'Deirdre of the Sorrows,' is in her fifties now, but when I met her recently I found that her voice is still as fresh, velvety and musical as when first she crossed the footlights of the Abbey in the exciting springtime of Yeats, Lady Gregory, the Fay Brothers and Synge himself. It was a brave group of young men and women—none of them older than twenty-five and none of them trained in the art of the theatre, but all of them united with one burning ambition—to have their own literary playhouse.

* *Irish Press* (Dublin) (21 Apr 1949) p. 4.

Sarah Allgood is the famous sister of Maire O'Neill, and, though they have had no immediate ancestor on the stage, there is in the family tree of four generations ago the name of Mary Haynes, well-known to the Dublin theatre of her day.

'There were four brothers and four sisters in my family of Allgood,' Maire told me. 'One brother is in the Civil Service in Dublin, one became a religious in an Irish monastery, and the other two were killed in the 1914–18 War. One of my sisters is here in London, one in Dublin, and of course Sarah has settled down in Hollywood.'

'Why did you change your name?' I asked.

'Oh, I wanted to be different to Sarah, of course, who kept the family name of Allgood. You know the dreams and ambitions of a young actress: she wants to be independent and different from everyone. I wanted to be different from Sarah, and to be on my own, to make my own fame and name, so I chose to be Maire O'Neill. . . . And here I am.'

* * *

I was anxious to speak about Synge, but Miss O'Neill's words on her quondam sweetheart were few but significant.

'What is there I cannot say about John? To me he was everything, in his work and personality. To-day he still remains the same for me. I have had no reason to change my opinion. Just as the rest of the world hasn't changed its opinion either. The history of the stage has made him immortal. He was one of the first of the Abbey Theatre writers. That is one of his greatnesses. But perhaps his greatness to me is wound up with the fact that for me he wrote his most famous plays, "The Playboy of the Western World" and "Deirdre of the Sorrows," when I was only eighteen.'

Before they could marry, John Millington Synge died at the very young age of thirty-nine. It took Maire O'Neill a long time to get over that blow, so that she did not marry till she came across to England in 1911 and met John Mair. . . .

Their son, John, became a writer, and his best book 'The Fourth Forger' dealing with the John Ireland forgeries of Shakespeare's works is still sought after especially in literary and dramatic circles. The son, John, died in a plane crash in 1942. The daughter, Pegeen, worked in publicity for Rank for two years, but gave it up in favour of lyric-writing.

I manœuvred the conversation back to our main topic, and Maire O'Neill continued:

'I left the Abbey in 1911 and came to London with the Company. We filled the theatres with "The Playboy" for two years. In New York in 1913 we played to crowded houses for six months in Lennox Robinson's "Whiteheaded Boy." Then we went south to Australia and stayed there for six months doing Sean O'Casey's "Juno and the Paycock." Incidentally, I was the first to televise "Juno" in this country. Since those early days I've paid another visit to America, in between playing all over Great Britain

and doing films. One great actor who has since become famous in films, Claude Rains, was with me in Carl Capek's "The Insect Play."'

'What advice would you give to aspiring actors and actresses?' I asked. I got a full reply. 'Join a good Repertory Company. Learn all that is to be known about every and any part. There is no reason why any girl or boy who has good natural ability and works hard in Repertory should not reach the top. But the most important thing is this—an actor or actress must have one essential quality, he or she must be an actor at heart. One must feel one is an actor within. Otherwise how can you *feel* your part? If you cannot do that, then all the gestures in the world will fail to put over the part. You will be a flop. An actor must have that capacity to feel the particular character he plays. Just as Delacroix revelled in the background of organ-music while painting his "Jacob and Heleodrus" in Saint Sulpice in Paris, so likewise must the sincere actor *feel* the moving power of his words in his heart, that same power, that verbal motivating music which finds *expression* in utterance by the lips. It's that kind of expression and feeling I tried to put into my part of Pegeen Mike as I speak to my lover Christy Mahon in "The Playboy." Take, for instance, the difficult part that begins

'"I'll say a strange man is a marvel with his mighty talk, but what's a squabble in your backyard? And the blow of a loy have taught me that there's a great difference between a gallous story and a dirty deed."

'These are difficult words to put over, requiring as I say a great technique in feeling and expression.'

* * *

Then we went on to speak about Radio Eireann where Maire O'Neill had done her old part in 'Riders to the Sea' a short time ago.

'Irish radio is practically lost to us here in England. We seldom if ever get it strong and clear enough to follow any one programme with comfort. We switch it on every day of course, but what do we get? A distant discord of whistles and crashes covering anything that might be news, plays or music. It is disgraceful. Of course I don't mean anything against the Radio Eireann authorities, but whoever has the means to give us an audible Radio Eireann here in England should do so. Why don't you broadcast from your new short-wave station and make Radio Eireann as dear in England as the B.B.C. is in Ireland?'

And that was Maire O'Neill.

NOTE

Molly Allgood ['Maire O'Neill'], the subject of this interview, joined the Abbey Theatre and became one of its leading actresses. For her, Synge created two of his most famous characters and wrote some of his most moving poetry. In 1906 he fell in love with her. In the Ireland of seventy years ago, however, the difference between them could hardly have been greater. He was fifteen years older, but his education and his class background provided a much more

formidable barrier. For a long time he was unwilling to tell his mother or his family about her. His unorthodoxy in religion and politics was one thing, but falling in love with a Roman Catholic, an actress and a former department-store salesgirl was something he thought they could never have tolerated. Synge and Molly became secretly engaged, but the wedding was postponed when he became seriously ill. See *Letters to Molly: John Millington Synge to Maire O'Neill 1906–1909*, ed. Ann Saddlemyer (Cambridge, Massachusetts: Harvard University Press, 1971), and Elizabeth Coxhead, 'Sally and Molly (Sara Allgood and Maire O'Neill)', *Daughters of Erin* (London: Secker and Warburg, 1965) pp. 167–224.

The Death of Synge*

W. B. YEATS

March 23.

Molly Allgood[1] came to-day to ask where I would be to-morrow, as Synge wishes to send for me if strong enough. He wants 'to make arrangements'. He is dying.[2] They have ceased to give him food. Should we close the Abbey or keep it open while he still lives? Poor Molly is going through her work as always. Perhaps that is best for her. I feel Synge's coming death less now than when he first became ill. I am used to the thought of it and I do not find that I pity him. I pity her. He is fading out of life. I felt the same when I saw M——[3] in the madhouse. I pitied his wife. He seemed already dead. One does not feel that death is evil when one meets it,—evil, I mean, for the one who dies. Our Daimon is silent as was that other before the death of Socrates. The wildest sorrow that comes at the thought of death is, I think, 'Ages will pass over and no one ever again look on that nobleness or that beauty'. What is this but to pity the living and to praise the dead?

XII

March 24.

Synge is dead. In the early morning he said to the nurse, 'It is no use fighting death any longer' and he turned over and died. I called at the hospital this afternoon and asked the assistant matron if he knew he was dying. She answered, 'He may have known it for weeks, but he would not have said so to anyone. He would have no fuss. He was like that.' She added, with emotion in her voice, 'We were devoted to him'.

XIII

March 28.

Mr. Stephens, Synge's brother-in-law, said he suffered no pain but only

* Extracted from *The Death of Synge; Extracts from a Diary Kept in 1909* (Dublin: Cuala Press, 1928), reprinted in *Autobiographies* (London: Macmillan, 1955) pp. 497–527.

great weakness. On Sunday he questioned the doctor and convinced himself that he was dying. He told his brother-in-law next day and was quite cheerful, even making jokes. In the evening he saw Molly and told her to be brave and sent her to me that I might arrange about his writings. On the morning when I heard of his death a heavy storm was blowing and I doubt not when he died that it had well begun. That morning Lady Gregory felt a very great depression and was certain that some evil was coming, but feared for her grandchild, feared it was going to be ill. On the other hand, my sister Lolly said at breakfast, 'I think it will be all right with Synge, for last night I saw a galley struggling with a storm and then it shot into calm and bright sunlight and I heard the keel grate on the shore'. One remembers the voyages to Tir-nan-oge,[4] certainly the voyages of souls after death to their place of peace.

XIV

I have been looking through his poems and have read once more that on page 21, 'I asked if I got sick and died'. Certainly they were there at the funeral, his 'idiot' enemies: A—— who against all regulations rushed up to the dressing-rooms during the *Playboy* riot to tell the actors they should not have played in so disgraceful a play; B—— who has always used his considerable influence with the company against Synge, and has spoken against him in public; there, too, were the feeble friends who pretended to believe but gave no help. And there was C—— whose obituary notice speaks of Synge's work as only important in promise, of the exaggeration of those who praise it, and then claims that its writer spent many hours a day with Synge in Paris (getting the date wrong by two years, however), with Synge who was proud and lonely, almost as proud of his old blood as of his genius, and had few friends. There was D——, the Secretary of the Society—it had sent a wreath—whose animosity had much to do with the attacks in *Sinn Fein*. It was, to quote E——, a funeral 'small but select'. A good friend of Synge's quoted to me:

> How shall the ritual then be read,
> The requiem how be sung
> By you, by yours the evil eye,
> By yours the Slanderous tongue,
> That did to death the innocence
> That died, and died so young?

Yet these men came, though but in remorse; they saw his plays, though but to dislike; they spoke his name, though but to slander. Well-to-do Ireland never saw his plays nor spoke his name. Was he ever asked to any country house but Coole?[5] Was he ever asked to a dinner-party? How often I have wished that he might live long enough to enjoy that communion with idle, charming and cultivated women which Balzac[6] in one of his dedications calls 'the chief consolation of genius'!

XV

In Paris Synge once said to me, 'We should unite stoicism, asceticism and ecstasy. Two of them have often come together, but the three never.'

XVI

I believe that some thing I said may have suggested 'I asked if I got sick and died'. S—— had frequently attacked his work while admitting him a man of genius. He attacked it that he might remain on good terms with the people about him. When Synge was in hospital to be operated upon, S—— was there too as a patient, and I told Synge that whenever I spoke of his illness to any man that man said, 'And isn't it sad about S——?' until I could stand it no longer and burst out with 'I hope he will die', and now, as someone said, I was 'being abused all over the town as without heart'. I had learned that people were calling continually to inquire how S—— was, but hardly anybody called to ask for Synge. Two or three weeks later Synge wrote this poem. Had my words set his mind running on the thought that fools flourish, more especially as I had prophesied that S—— would flourish, and in my mood at the moment it seemed that for S—— to be operated on at the same time with Synge was a kind of insolence? S——'s illness did, indeed, win for him so much sympathy that he came out to lucrative and honourable employment, and now when playing golf he says with the English accent he has acquired of late, to some player who needs a great man's favour, 'I know him well, I will say a word in that quarter'.

The Irish weekly papers notice Synge's death with short and for the most part grudging notices. There was an obscure Gaelic League singer[7] who was a leader of the demonstration against the *Playboy*. He died on the same day. *Sinn Fein* notices both deaths in the same article[8] and gives three-fourths of it to the rioter. For Synge it has but grudging words, as was to be expected.

Molly tells me that Synge went to see Stephen MacKenna and his wife before going into hospital and said good-bye with 'You will never see me again'.

XVII

CELEBRATIONS

1. He was one of those unmoved souls in whom there is a perpetual 'Last Day', a perpetual trumpeting and coming up for judgment.
2. He did not speak to men and women, asking judgment, as lesser writers do; but knowing himself part of judgment he was silent.
3. We pity the living and not such dead as he. He has gone upward out of his ailing body into the heroical fountains. We are parched by time.
4. He had the knowledge of his coming death and was cheerful to the

end, even joking a little when that end had all but come. He had no need of our sympathies. It was as though we and the things about us died away from him and not he from us.

XVIII

DETRACTIONS

He had that egotism of the man of genius which Nietzsche compares to the egotism of a woman with child. Neither I nor Lady Gregory had ever a compliment from him. After *Hyacinth*[9] Lady Gregory went home the moment the curtain fell, not waiting for the congratulation of friends, to get his supper ready. He was always ailing and weakly. All he said of the triumphant *Hyacinth* was, 'I expected to like it better'. He had under charming and modest manners, in almost all things of life, a complete absorption in his own dream. I have never heard him praise any writer, living or dead, but some old French farce-writer. For him nothing existed but his thought. He claimed nothing for it aloud. He never said any of those self-confident things I am enraged into saying, but one knew that he valued nothing else. He was too confident for self-assertion. I once said to George Moore,[10] 'Synge has always the better of you, for you have brief but ghastly moments during which you admit the existence of other writers; Synge never has'. I do not think he disliked other writers—they did not exist. One did not think of him as an egotist. He was too sympathetic in the ordinary affairs of life and too simple. In the arts he knew no language but his own.

I have often envied him his absorption as I have envied Verlaine[11] his vice. Can a man of genius make that complete renunciation of the world necessary to the full expression of himself without some vice or some deficiency? You were happy or at least blessed, 'blind old man of Scio's rocky isle'.

NOTES

1. For a note on Molly Allgood see p. 73.
2. In 1908 exploratory surgery revealed that the growth in Synge's side was inoperable. In early 1909 he entered the Elpis Nursing Home, Lower Mount Street, Dublin, where he died soon after on 24 March 1909.
3. MacGregor Mathers, Yeats's friend who initiated him into a society called the Golden Dawn.
4. Literally, land of the youth, the Gaelic Elysium of pre-Christian Ireland.
5. It was W. B. Yeats who, in 1898, suggested that Lady Gregory should ask Synge to stay for a while in her house at Coole Park, Gort, County Galway, twenty-two miles from Galway City. Today almost nothing remains of Lady Gregory's 'modest white-fronted house rather like a large Italian farmhouse', as Joseph Hone described it in *W. B. Yeats* (New York, 1943) p. 144. See Anne Gregory, *Me and Nu: Childhood at Coole* (Gerrards Cross, Buckinghamshire: Colin Smythe, 1970).

6. Honoré de Balzac (1799–1850), considered the greatest novelist of France. His work is essentially romantic, but so detailed as to make it appear that he is a realist.
7. John Lawless.
8. 'The Dead', *Sinn Fein* (Dublin), III, no. 152 (3 Apr 1909) 1.
9. *Hyacinth Halvey,* a comedy in one act by Lady Gregory, was first produced at the Abbey Theatre on 19 February 1906.
10. For a note on George Moore see p. 104.
11. Paul Verlaine (1844–96), French poet and a leading Symbolist.

John M. Synge*

JOHN MASEFIELD

I first met John M. Synge at the room of a mutual friend,[1] up two pairs of stairs, in an old house in Bloomsbury, on a Monday night of January, 1903.[2] When I entered the room, he was sitting in a rush-bottomed chair, talking to a young man just down from Oxford. My host introduced me, with the remark that he wanted us to know each other.

Synge stood up to shake hands with me. He was of the middle height, about five feet eight or nine. My first impression of him was of a dark, grave face, with a great deal in it; changing from the liveliness of conversation to a gravity of scrutiny. After we had shaken hands, I passed to the other end of the room to greet other friends. We did not speak to each other again that night.

When I sat at the other end of the room my chair was opposite Synge's chair. Whenever I raised my eyes I saw him, and wondered who he could be. Disordered people look disordered, unusual people look unusual. A youth with long hair, a velvet coat, extravagant manners, and the other effeminacies of emptiness looks the charlatan he is. Synge gave one from the first the impression of a strange personality. He was of a dark type of Irishman, though not black-haired. Something in his air gave one the fancy that his face was dark from gravity. Gravity filled the face and haunted it, as though the man behind were forever listening to life's case before passing judgment. It was 'a dark, grave face, with a great deal in it.' The hair was worn neither short nor long. The moustache was rather thick and heavy. The lower jaw, otherwise clean-shaven, was made remarkable by a tuft of hair, too small to be called a goatee, upon the lower lip. The head was of a good size. There was nothing niggardly, nothing abundant about it. The face was pale, the cheeks were rather drawn. In my memory they were rather seamed and old-looking. The eyes were at once

---

* *Contemporary Review* (London) IC (Apr 1911) 470–8, reprinted as *John M. Synge: A Few Personal Recollections, with Biographical Notes* (Dublin: Cuala Press, 1915).

smoky and kindling. The mouth, not well seen below the moustache, had a great play of humour on it. But for this humorous mouth, the kindling in the eyes, and something not robust in his build, he would have been more like a Scotchman than an Irishman.

I remember wondering if he were Irish. His voice, very guttural and quick, with a kind of lively bitterness in it, was of a kind of Irish voice new to me at that time. I had known a good many Irish people; but they had all been vivacious and picturesque, rapid in intellectual argument, and vague about life. There was nothing vivacious, picturesque, rapid or vague about Synge. The rush-bottomed chair next to him was filled by talker after talker, but Synge was not talking, he was answering. When someone spoke to him he answered with the grave Irish courtesy. He offered nothing of his own. When the talk became general he was silent. Sometimes he went to a reddish earthenware pot upon the table, took out a cigarette and lit it at a candle. Then he sat smoking, pushed back a little from the circle, gravely watching. Sometimes I heard his deep, grave voice assenting 'Ye-es, ye-es,' with meditative boredom. Sometimes his little finger flicked off the ash on to the floor. His manner was that of a man too much interested in the life about him to wish to be more than a spectator. His interest was in life, not in ideas. He was new to that particular kind of life. Afterwards, when I had come to know him, I heard him sum up every person there with extraordinary point and sparkle. Often since then, eager to hear more of my friend, I have asked men who met him casually for a report of him. So often they have said, 'He was a looker-on at life.' 'He came in and sat down and looked on.' 'He gave nothing in return.' 'He never talked, he only listened.' 'I never got much out of Synge.' 'I never got to the real Synge.' 'I was never conscious of what he felt.' 'Sometimes I felt that there was nothing in him.' 'I never knew him respond.' 'I never knew him do or say anything to suggest what he was in himself.' When I hear these phrases, I know that those who utter them really met Synge. His place was outside the circle, gravely watching, gravely summing up, with a brilliant malice, the fools and wise ones inside.

A week, or perhaps a fortnight, later, I met him again at the same place, among the same people. He was talking brightly and charmingly to a woman. Men usually talk their best to women. When I turn over my memories of him, it seems that his grave courtesy was only gay when he was talking to women. His talk to women had a lightness and charm. It was sympathetic; never self-assertive, as the hard, brilliant Irish intellect so often is.[3] He liked people to talk to him. He liked to know the colours of people's minds. He liked to be amused. His merriest talk was like playing catch with an apple of banter, which one afterwards ate and forgot.

He never tried to be brilliant. I never heard him say a brilliant thing. He said shrewd things. I do not know what he could have done if stirred to talk. Few people born out of old, sunny countries talk well. I never heard him engaged with a brilliant talker, either man or woman. He told me that

once, in Paris, he had gone to hear a brilliant talker—a French poet, now dead. It was like him that he did not speak to the talker. 'We sat round on chairs and the great man talked.'

During the evening, I spoke a few words to Synge about some Irish matter. We pushed back our chairs out of the circle and discussed it. I did not know at that time that he was a writer. I knew by name most of the writers in the Irish movement. Synge was not one of the names. I thought that he must be at work on the political side. I wronged him in this. He never played any part in politics: politics did not interest him. He was the only Irishman I have ever met who cared nothing for either the political or the religious issue. He had a prejudice against one Orange district, because the people in it were dour. He had a prejudice against one Roman Catholic district, because the people in it were rude. Otherwise his mind was untroubled. Life was what interested him. He would have watched a political or religious riot with gravity, with pleasure in the spectacle, and malice for the folly. He would have taken no side, and felt no emotion, except a sort of pity when the losers could go on no longer. The question was nothing to him. All that he asked for was to hear what it made people say and to see what it made people do.

Towards one in the morning, our host asked Synge and me to sup with him. We foraged in the pantry, and found some eggs, but nothing in which to cook them. Our host said that he would try a new trick, of boiling eggs in a paper box. We were scornful about it, thinking it impossible. He brought out paper, made a box (with some difficulty), filled it with water, and boiled an egg in it. Synge watched the task with the most keen interest. 'You've done it,' he said. 'I never thought you would.' Afterwards he examined the paper box. I suppose he planned to make one in Aran in the summer. While we supped, our host chaffed us both for choosing to eat cold meats when we might have had nice hot eggs. It was at this supper that I first came to know the man.

When we got into the street, we found that we lodged within a few minutes' walk of each other. We walked together to our lodgings. He said that he had been for a time in Aran, that he had taken some photographs there, and that he would be pleased to show them to me, if I would call upon him later in the morning. He said that he had just come to London from Paris, and that he found Bloomsbury strange after the Quartier Latin. He was puzzled by the talk of the clever young men from Oxford. 'That's a queer way to talk. They all talk like that. I wonder what makes them talk like that? I suppose they're always stewing over dead things.'

Synge lodged in a front room on the second floor of No. 4, Handel Street, Bloomsbury. It was a quiet house in a quiet, out-of-the-way street. His room there was always very clean and tidy. The people made him very comfortable. Afterwards, in 1907, during his last visit to London, he lodged there again, in the same room. I called upon him there in the afternoon of the day on which I last saw him.

When I first called upon him, I found him at his type-writer, hard at work. He was making a fair copy of one of his two early one-act plays, then just finished. His type-writer was a small portable machine; I do not know the make.[4] He was the only writer I have ever known who composed direct upon a type-writing machine. I have often seen him at work upon it. Sometimes, when I called to ask him to come for a walk, he had matter to finish off before we could start. He worked rather slowly and very carefully, sitting very upright. He composed slowly. He wrote and re-wrote his plays many times. I remember that on this first occasion the table had a pile of type-written drafts upon it, as well as a few books, one or two of them by M. Pierre Loti.[5] He thought M. Loti the best living writer of prose. There are marks of M. Loti's influence in the Aran book. Much of the Aran manuscript was on the table at that time. Synge asked me to wait for a few minutes while he finished the draft at which he was working. He handed me a black tobacco-pouch and a packet of cigarette-papers. While I rolled a cigarette he searched for his photographs and at last handed them to me. They were quarter-plate prints in a thick bundle. There must have been fifty of them. They were all of the daily life of Aran; women carrying kelp, men in hookers, old people at their doors, a crowd at the landing-place, men loading horses, people of vivid character, pigs and children playing together, &c. As I looked at them he explained them or commented on them in a way which made all sharp and bright. His talk was best when it was about life or the ways of life. His mind was too busy with the life to be busy with the affairs or the criticism of life. His talk was all about men and women and what they did and what they said when life excited them. His mind was perhaps a little like Shakespeare's. We do not know what Shakespeare thought: I do not know what Synge thought. I don't believe anybody knew, or thinks he knows.

'There was something very nice about Synge.' The friend who said this to me, added that 'though the plays are cynical, he was not cynical in himself.' I do not feel that the plays are cynical. They seem heartless at first sight. The abundant malicious joy in them gives them an air of cruelty. But in the plays, Synge did with his personality as he did in daily life. He buried his meaning deep. He covered his tragedy with mockeries.

More than a year ago a friend asked me what sort of man Synge was. I answered, 'a perfect companion.' The other day I saw that another friend, who knew him better than I, had described him as 'the best companion.' After that first day, when I called upon him at his room, we met frequently. We walked long miles together,[6] generally from Bloomsbury to the river, along the river to Vauxhall, and back by Westminster to Soho. We sometimes dined together at a little French restaurant, called the Restaurant des Gourmets. The house still stands; but it has now grown to five times the size. The place where Synge and I used to sit has now been improved away. We spent happy hours there, talking, rolling cigarettes, and watching the life. 'Those were great days,' he used to say. He was the

best companion for that kind of day.

Our talk was always about life. When we talked about writers (modern French and ancient English writers) it was not about their writings that we talked, but about the something kindling in them, which never got expressed. His theory of writing was this:— 'No good writer can ever be translated.' He used to quote triumphantly:—

'As any she belied with false compare.'

'How would you put that into French?' he asked.

He never talked about himself. He often talked of his affairs, his money, his little room in Paris, his meetings with odd characters, &c., but never of himself. He had wandered over a lot of Europe. He was silent about all that.

Very rarely, and then by chance, when telling of the life in Aran, or of some strange man in the train or in the steamer, he revealed little things about himself:—

'They asked me to fiddle to them, so that they might dance.'

'Do you play, then?'

'I fiddle a little. I try to learn something different for them every time. The last time I learned to do conjuring tricks. They'd get tired of me if I didn't bring something new. I'm thinking of learning the penny whistle before I go again.'

I never heard him mention his early life nor what he endured in his struggles to find a form. I believe he never spoke about his writings, except to say that he wrote them slowly, many times over. His talk was always about vivid, picturesque, wild life. He took greater joy in what some frantic soul from Joyce's country said when the policeman hit him than in anything of his own. He found no vivid life in England. He disliked England. I think he only knew London. Afterwards he stayed for a couple of weeks in Devonshire. London is a place where money can be made and spent. Devonshire is a place where elderly ladies invite retired naval officers to tea. England lies further to the north. He was never in any part of England where the country life is vigorous and picturesque. He believed England to be all suburb, like the 'six counties overhung with smoke.'

Soon after our first meeting I was present at his first success. His two early plays, *Riders to the Sea* and *The Shadow of the Glen,* were read aloud to about a dozen friends at the rooms of one [7] who was always most generously helpful to writers not yet sure of their road. A lady [8] read the plays very beautifully. Afterwards we all [9] applauded. Synge learned his *métier* that night. Until then, all his work had been tentative and in the air. After that, he went forward, knowing what he could do.

For two or three months I met Synge almost daily. Presently he went back to Ireland (I believe to Aran) and I to 'loath'd Devonshire.' I met him again, later in the year. During the next few years, though he was not often in town, I met him fairly often whenever the Irish players came to

London. Once I met him for a few days together in Dublin. He was to have stayed with me both in London and in Ireland; but on both occasions his health gave way, and the visit was never paid. I remember sitting up talking with him through the whole of one winter night (in 1904). Later, when the Rokeby Velasquez[10] was being talked of, I went with him to see the picture. We agreed that it was the kind of picture people paint when mind is beginning to get languid. After we had seen the picture I walked with him to his hotel (the Kenilworth Hotel), talking about Irish art, which he thought was the kind of art people make when mind has been languid for a long time. I never saw him angry. I never saw him vexed. I never heard him utter a hasty or an unkind word. I saw him visibly moved once to sadness, when some one told him how tourists had spoiled the country people in a part of Ireland. The Irish country people are simple and charming. Tourists make them servile, insolent, and base. 'The Irish are easily corrupted,' he said, 'because they are so simple. When they're corrupted, they're hard, they're rude, they're everything that's bad. But they're only that where the low-class tourists go, from America, and Glasgow, and Liverpool and these places.' He seldom praised people, either for their work or for their personality. When he spoke of mutual friends he generally quoted a third person. When he uttered a personal judgment it was always short, like 'He's a great fellow,' or 'He's a grand fellow,' or 'Nobody in Ireland understands how big he is.'

On one occasion (I think in 1906) we lunched together (at the Vienna Café). He told me with huge delight about his adventures in the wilds. He had lodged in a cabin far from the common roads. There was no basin in his bed-room. He asked for one, so that he might wash. The people brought him a wooden box, worn smooth with much use. In the morning he was roused by his host with the cry, 'Have you washed yourself yet? Herself is wanting the box to make up the bread in.'

I remember asking him what sensations an author had when his play was being performed for the first time. 'I sit still in my box,' he said, 'and curse the actors.'

He was in a very gay mood that afternoon, though his health was fast failing. He spoke with his usual merry malice about his throat. With the trouble in his throat he could not tell when he would be in England again. He was only in England once more. That was in late May or early June, 1907, when the Irish players gave a few performances at the Kingsway Theatre.[11] I met him in the foyer of the theatre just before the first London performance of *The Playboy of the Western World*. I had some talk with him then. During the performance I saw him in his box, 'sitting still' as he said, watching with the singular grave intensity with which he watched life. It struck me then that he was the only person there sufficiently simple to be really interested in living people; and that it was this simplicity which gave him his charm. He found the life in a man very well worth wonder, even though the man were a fool, or a knave, or just down from Oxford. At the

end of the play I saw him standing in his box, gravely watching the actors as the curtain rose and again rose during the applause. Presently he turned away to speak to the lady who had read his plays on the night of his first success. The play was loudly applauded. Some people behind me—a youth and a girl—began to hiss. I remember thinking that they resembled the bird they imitated.

I only saw Synge on two other occasions. I met him at a dinner party, but had no talk with him, and I called upon him at his old lodgings in Handel Street. He said:—

'Doesn't it seem queer to you to be coming back here?'
'It seems only the other day that we were here.'
'Those were great days.'
'I wish we could have them again.'
'Ah,' he said, laughing his hard laugh, half a cough,

> 'Nature brings not back the mastodon,
> Nor we those times.'

Presently he told me that he had been writing poetry. He handed me a type-written copy of a ballad, and asked me what I thought of it. I told him that I felt the want of an explanatory stanza near the beginning. 'Yes,' he said; 'But I can't take your advice, because then it would not be quite my own.' He told me the wild, picturesque story (of a murder in Connaught) which had inspired the ballad.[12] His relish of the savagery made me feel that he was a dying man clutching at life, and clutching most wildly at violent life, as the sick man does. We went out shortly afterwards, and got into a cab, and drove to the Gourmets, and ate our last meal together. He was going to the theatre after dinner; I had to go out of town. After dinner we got into another cab. He said he would give me a lift towards my station. We drove together along the Strand, talking of the great times we would have and of the jolly times we had had. None of our many talks together was happier than the last. I felt in my heart as we drove that I should never see him again. Our last talk together was to be a happy one.

He was later than he thought. He could not come all the way to my station. He had to turn off to his theatre. At the top of Fleet Street hill we shook hands and said 'So long' to each other. The cab drew up just outside the office of a sporting newspaper. I got out, and raised my hand to him. He raised his in his grave way. The cab swung round and set off westwards, and that was the end.

When I heard of his death I felt that his interest in life would soon get itself into another body, and come here again to look on and listen. When a life ends, it is a sign that Nature's purpose in that life is over. When a personality has passed from us it is a sign that life has no further need of it. What that personality did may matter. What that personality was does not matter. Man's task is to leave the dead alone. Life would be finer if we did not drag that caddis-worm's house of the past behind us.

I have not set down all my memories of him. Much of what he told and said to me was told and said in the confidence of friendship. I have set down only a few odd fragments to show those who care to know what sort of a man he was. Lies and lives will be written of him; plenty of both. Enough should be said to defeat the malice and stupidity of detractors. Those who want to know what he was in himself should read the poems. The poems are the man speaking. They are so like him that to read them is to hear him. The couplet—

> 'But they are rotten (I ask their pardon),
> And we've the sun on rock and garden.'

gives me, whenever I read it, the feeling that he is in the room, looking up with his hard, quick guttural laugh and kindling eyes, from the rolling of a cigarette. The issue of *Samhain* for December, 1904, contains a portrait of him by Mr. J. B. Yeats. It is difficult to believe that there can be any portrait more like him.

NOTES

John Masefield (1878–1967), English poet, playwright and fiction writer; Poet Laureate (from 1930); member of Order of Merit (1935). Among his notable works are *Salt Water Ballads* (1902), *A Mainsail Haul* (stories of the sea; 1905), *Captain Margaret* (romance; 1908), *The Tragedy of Nan and Other Plays* (1910), *The Tragedy of Pompey the Great* (1910); the verse narratives *The Everlasting Mercy* (1911), *The Window in the Bye Street* (1912) and *Dauber* (1913); *The Story of a Roundhouse and Other Poems* (1912), *Philip the King* (drama; 1914), *Gallipoli* (prose sketches, 1916) *Reynard the Fox* (narrative poems; 1919); novels of adventure, as *Sard Harker* (1924), *Odtaa* (1926), *Dead Ned* (1938) and *Live and Kicking Ned* (1939); *Basilissa* (fictional biography of Empress Theodora; 1940); *Generation Risen* (poems; 1942). Yeats was a close friend of Masefield, of whose departure for a post in the country he once said: 'When he is gone I shall be gloomy enough.' It was Masefield who caused the *Manchester Guardian* to commission a number of articles from Synge, the first of which was first published on 24 January 1905. Synge particularly liked Masefield, and they became close enough friends for Synge to show him some of his poems long before he admitted to Yeats that he was still writing verse.

1. W. B. Yeats, who was living at 18 Woburn Buildings, a stone-flagged alley or passage running eastward from the since obliterated Woburn Place.

2. Until he arrived in London on 9 January 1903 to seek publication for his Aran book and his plays, Synge had met relatively few writers. While he was very much a part of the W. B. Yeats—Lady Gregory circle in Ireland, his only other literary friends were Richard Best and Stephen MacKenna. Now, however, once he had settled into his boarding-house in London, he found himself reading his plays aloud to literary gatherings both in Lady Gregory's rooms and those of Yeats, and becoming acquainted with Arthur Symons, G. K. Chesterton, John Masefield and others.

3. 'With women he was always more at ease than with men. He found himself able to entertain them with his wit and became in their company far more articulate than he ever was with men.'—Robin Skelton, *J. M. Synge and His World* (London: Thames and Hudson, 1971) p. 33.

4. It was a 'Blick' (Blickensderfer), which he had bought for £8 in Dublin.

5. For a note on Pierre Loti see p. 69.

6. It is to Synge that Masefield refers in his poem, 'Biography':

  And now I miss that friend who used to walk
  Home to my lodgings with me, deep in talk

7. Lady Gregory. The rooms were in Queen Anne's Mansions, London, S.W.
8. The lady was Lady Gregory. For a note on her see p. 7.
9. Arthur Symons, R. Brinsley Johnson and Florence Farr were present.
10. Rokeyby Venus (c. 1651), the painting by Diego Velázquez (1599–1660), the painter who is acknowledged as one of the giants of Western art.
11. The Irish players started their performances on 10 June 1907 at the Great Queen Street Theatre and not, as John Masefield says, at the Kingsway Theatre.
12. 'The 'Mergency Man'. Synge was disturbed because poetry had become removed from the interests and activities of the majority of people; and he tried to close the breach. On several occasions he discussed the problem with Masefield, and the two writers seem to have felt that the re-creation of ballad poetry was both desirable and possible.

Synge*

LADY GREGORY

I first saw J. M. Synge in the North Island of Aran. I was staying there gathering folk-lore, talking to the people, and felt quite angry when I passed another outsider walking here and there, talking also to the people. I was jealous of not being alone on the island among the fishers and seaweed gatherers. I did not speak to the stranger, nor was he inclined to speak to me; he also looked on me as an intruder, I only heard his name. But a little later in the summer Mr. Yeats, who was staying with me at Coole, had a note from Synge saying he was in Aran. They had met in Paris, Yeats had written of him from there: 'He is really a most excellent man. He lives in a little room which he has furnished himself; he is his own servant. He works very hard and is learning Breton; he will be a very useful scholar.'

  I asked him here[1] and we became friends at once. I said of him in a letter: 'One never has to rearrange one's mind to talk to him.' He was quite direct, sincere and simple, not only a good listener, but too good a one, not speaking much in general society. His fellow guests at Coole always liked him, and he was pleasant and genial with them, though once, when he had come straight from life on a wild coast, he confessed that a somewhat warlike English lady in the house was 'Civilisation in its most violent form.' For there could be a sharp edge to his wit, as when he said of a certain actress (not Mrs. Campbell) whose modern methods he disliked, she had turned Yeats' *Deirdre* into 'the Second Mrs. Conchubar,' and once, when

---

* *English Review* (London) XIII (Mar 1913) 556–66, reprinted, with variations, from *Our Irish Theatre* (London and New York: G. P. Putman, 1913) pp. 120–39.

awaking from the anaesthetic after one of those hopeless operations, the first words that could be understood were, 'Those damned English can't even swear without vulgarity.' He sent me later, when we had been long working at the theatre, some review of his work from a German newspaper: 'What gives me a sympathy with this new man is that he does not go off into sentimentality. Behind this legend I see a laughing face, then he raises his eyebrows in irony and laughs again. Herr Synge may not be a dramatist, he may not be a great poet, but he has something that I like in him, a thing that for many good Germans is a book with seven seals, that is, Humour.'

He writes a note with this: 'I'd like to quote about "Humour," but I don't want to tell Dublin I'm maybe no dramatist, that wouldn't do.' Of his other side, Mr. J. B. Yeats wrote to me: 'Coleridge said that all Shakespeare's characters, from Macbeth to Dogberry, were "ideal realities." His comedies "poetry as an unlimited jest," and his tragedies "poetry in deepest earnest." Had he seen Synge's plays he would have called them "poetry in unlimited sadness."'

While staying with us he hardly looked at a newspaper. He seemed to look on politics and reforms with a sort of tolerant indifference, though he spoke once of something that has happened as 'the greatest tragedy since Parnell's death.' He told me that the people of the play he was writing often seemed the real people among whom he was living, and I think his dreamy look came from this. When here he spent a good deal of time wandering in our woods, where many shy creatures still find their home, marten cats and squirrels and otters and badgers, and by the lake where wild swans come and go. He said he had given up wearing the black clothes he had worn for a while, when they were a fashion with writers, thinking they were not in harmony with Nature, which is so sparing in the use of the harsh colour of the raven. Simple things always pleased him. In his long illness, at a Dublin Hospital where I went to see him every day, he would ask for every detail of a search I was making for a couple of Irish terrier puppies to bring home, and laugh at my adventures again and again. And when I described to him the place where I had found the puppies at last, a little house in a suburb, with a long garden stretching into wild fields with a view of the hills beyond, he was excited, and said that it was just such a Dublin home as he had wanted, and had been sure was somewhere to be found. He asked me at this time about a village on the Atlantic coast where I had stayed for a while in rooms over a post office, and where he had hoped he might go for his convalescence instead of to Germany, which had been arranged for him. I said in talking of it that I felt more and more the time wasted that was not spent in Ireland, and he said: 'That is just my feeling.'

When my *Cuchulain of Muirthemme*[2] came out he said to Mr. Yeats he had been amazed to find in it the dialect he had been trying to master. He wrote to me: 'Your Cuchulain is a part of my daily bread'; I say this with a little pride, for I was the first to use the Irish idiom as it is spoken, with intention and with belief in it. Dr. Hyde[3] has used it with fine effect in his

'Love Songs of Connacht,' but alas! gave it up afterwards in deference to some Dublin editor.

Also I must be proud of any word of praise from Synge, for he did not use many. Mr. Yeats writes, and expects me to feel personally flattered: 'By the way, Synge is becoming quite complimentary. He says your Mancini[4] portrait is the greatest since Rembrandt.'[5] And he writes in his diary a few days after Synge's death: 'He had that egotism of the man of genius which Nietzsche compares to the egotism of a woman with child. I never knew what he thought of my work. . . . After the first performance of *Hyacinth Halvey*, Lady Gregory went the very moment the play was over to get supper for him, for he was ailing at the time, not waiting for the congratulation of friends. All he said of the triumphant *Hyacinth* was: "I expected to like it better." He had under charming and modest manners in almost all things of life complete absorption in his own dream. I have never heard him praise any writer, living or dead, but some old French farce writers, for here nothing existed but his thought. He claimed nothing for it aloud, he never said any of those confident things I say too often when angry, but one knew that he valued nothing else. He was too confident for self-assertion. I once said to George Moore: "Synge has always the better of you, for you have brief but ghastly moments in which you admit the existence of other writers, Synge never has." I do not think he disliked other writers, they did not exist. One did not think him an egotist, he was too sympathetic in the ordinary affairs of life and too simple. In the arts he knew no language but his own.'

The rich, abundant speech of the people was a delight to him. He wrote to me after his first visit: 'I had a very prosperous journey up from Gort. At Athenry an old Irish-speaking wanderer made my acquaintance. He claims to be the best singer in England, Ireland and America. One night he says he sang a song at Moate, and a friend of his heard the words in Athenry. He was so much struck by the event that he had himself examined by one who knew, and found that his singing did not come out of his lungs, but out of his heart, which is a "winged heart!"'

At the time of his first visit to Coole he had written some poems, not very good for the most part, and a play[6] which was not good at all. I read it again after his death when, according to his written wish, helping Mr. Yeats and sorting out the work to be published or set aside, and again it seemed but of slight merit. But a year later he brought us his two plays, *The Shadow of the Glen*[7] and the *Riders to the Sea*,[8] both masterpieces, both perfect in their way. He had gathered emotion, the driving force he needed from his life among the people, and it was the working in dialect that had set free his style.

He was anxious to publish his book on Aran and these two plays, and so having something to add to that 'Forty pounds a year and a new suit when I am too shabby,' he used with a laugh to put down as his income. He wrote to me from Paris in February, 1902: 'I don't know what part of Europe you

may be in now, but I suppose this will reach you if I send it to Coole. I want to tell you the evil fate of my Aran book and ask your advice. It has been to two publishers, to Grant Richards, who was sympathetic, though he refused it as he said it could not be a commercial success, and to Fisher Unwin, who was inclined to be scornful.

'Now that you have seen the book, do you think there would be any chance of Alfred Nutt taking it up? I am afraid he is my only chance, but I don't know whether there is any possibility of getting him to bring out a book of the kind at his own expense, as, after all, there is very little folk-lore in it.'

I took the book to London and had it re-typed, for he, like myself, typed his own manuscript, and this was very faint and rubbed, and both Mr. Yeats and I took it to publishers, but they would not take it. Writing in March, '03, he says: 'My play came back from the *Fortnightly* as not suitable for their purposes. And I don't think that Brinsley Johnson intends to bring out the Aran book. I saw him on my way home, but he seemed hopelessly undecided, saying one minute he liked it very much, and that it might be a great success, and that he wanted to be in touch with the Irish movement, and then going off in the other direction and fearing that it might fall perfectly flat! Finally he asked me to let him consider it a little longer.'

I was no more successful. I wrote to Mr. Yeats, who was in America: 'I went to Bullen[9] about the music for your book. . . . I think I told you he had never opened the Synge MS. and said he would rather have nothing to do with it. Masefield[10] has it now.' Then I had a note: 'Dear Lady Gregory, I saw Newbolt yesterday and spoke to him about Synge's new play (*Riders to the Sea*), which struck me as being in some ways even better than the other. He has promised to read it if it is sent to him, though he does not much care for plays. Will you post it to the Editor, *Monthly Review*. . . . Yours very truly, Arthur Symons.'[11] Nothing came of that, and in December Synge writes: 'I am delighted to find that there is a prospect of getting the book out at last, and equally grateful for the trouble you have taken with it. I am writing to Masefield to-day to thank him, and ask him by all means to get Mathews to do as he proposes. Do you think if he brings out the plays in the Spring I should add *The Tinker*? I was getting on well with the blind people (in *Well of the Saints*) till about a month ago, when I suddenly got ill with influenza and a nasty attack on my lung. I am getting better now, but I cannot work yet satisfactorily, so I hardly know when the play is likely to be finished. There is no use trying to hurry on with a thing of that sort when one is not in the mood.'

Yet the Aran book was not published, after all, till 1907, when his name had already gone up. *The Shadow of the Glen* and the *Riders to the Sea* were published by Mr. Elkin Mathews in 1905. *Riders to the Sea* had already been published in *Samhain*,[12] the little annual of our theatre, edited by Mr. Yeats. And in America a friend of ours and of the Theatre had printed some of the plays in a little edition of fifty copies, thus saving the copyright.

It was of Synge and of others as well as myself I thought when, in dedicating a book to John Quinn when I was in America last winter, I wrote: 'Best friend, best helper these half score years on this side of the sea.'

When Synge had joined us in the management of the Theatre he took his share of the work,[13] and though we were all amateurs then, we got on somehow or other. He writes about a secretary we had sent for him to report on: 'He seems very willing, and I think may do very well if he does not take fright at us. He still thinks it was a terrible thing for Yeats to suggest that Irish people should sell their souls and for you to put His Sacred Majesty James II. into the barrel. He should be very useful in working up an audience; an important part of our work that we have rather neglected. By the way, the annual meeting of our company must be held, I suppose, before the year is up. It would be well to have it before we pay off Ryan,[14] as otherwise we shall all be sitting about looking with curiosity and awe at the balance sheet.'

He went on bravely with his work, always fighting against ill-health.

'Feb. 15, '06. Many thanks for the MS. of *Le Medicin*.[15] I think he is entirely admirable and is certain to go well. This is just a line to acknowledge the MS. as I suppose I shall see you in a day or two.

'My play has made practically no way since, as I have been down for ten days with bronchitis. My lung is not touched, however, and I have got off well considering. I hope I shall be all right by next week.'

(About same date): 'I am pleased with the way my play is going, but I find it quite impossible to rush through with it now, so I rather think I shall take it and the typewriter to some place in Kerry where I could work. By doing so I would get some sort of holiday and still avoid dropping the play again—which is a rather dangerous process. If I do this I will be beyond posts.... If I do not get a good summer I generally pay for it in the winter in extra bouts of influenza and all its miseries.'

'August 12, '06. I shall be very glad, thanks, to go down and read you my play (*The Playboy*) if it is finished in time, but there is still a great deal to do. I have had a very steady week's work since last Sunday and have made good way, but my head is getting very tired, working in hot weather takes a lot out of me.'

'November 25, '06. I have had rather a worse attack than I expected when I wrote my last note, but I am much better now, and out as usual. One of my lungs, however, has been a little touched, so I shall have to be careful for a while. Would it be possible to put off *The Playboy* for a couple of weeks? I am afraid if I went to work at him again now, and then rehearsed all December, I would be very likely to knock up badly before I was done with him. My doctor says I may do so if it is *necessary*, but he advises me to take a couple of weeks' rest if it can be managed. That cousin[16] of mine who etches is over here now and he wants me to stay with him for a fortnight in a sort of country house he has in Surrey, so if you think the *Playboy* can be put off, I will go across on Thursday or Friday and get back in time to see the

Shadowy Waters[17] and get the *Playboy* under way for January. What do you think? If so, I would like to read the third act of *Playboy* to you before I go, and then make final changes, while I am away, as I shall have a quiet time.'

He worked very hard at the *Playboy*, altering it a good deal as he went on. He had first planned the opening act in the ploughed field, where the quarrel between Christy and his father took place. But when he thought of the actual stage he could not see any possible side wings for that 'wide, windy corner of high, distant hills.' He had also talked of the return of the father being at the very door of the chapel where Christy was to wed Pegeen; but in the end all took place within the one cottage room. We all tried at that time to write for as little scene-shifting as might be, for economy of scenery and of stage-hands.

In October, 1906, he writes to Mr. Yeats: 'My play, though in its last agony, is not finished, and I cannot promise it for any definite day. It is more than likely that when I read it to you and Fay there will be little things to alter that have escaped me, and with my stuff it takes time to get even half a page of new dialogue fully into key with what goes before it. The play, I think, will be one of the longest we have done, and in places extremely difficult. If we said the 19th, I could only have six or seven full rehearsals, which would not, I am quite sure, be enough. . . . I am very sorry, but what is to be done?' Then to me in November: 'May I read the *Playboy* to you and Yeats and Fay some time to-morrow, Saturday or Monday according as it suits you all? A little verbal correction is still necessary, and one or two structural points may need—I fancy do need revision, but I would like to have your opinions on it before I go on further.'

I remember his bringing the play to us in Dublin, but he was too hoarse to read it, and it was read by Mr. Fay. We were almost bewildered by its abundance and fantasy, but we felt—and Mr. Yeats said very plainly—that there was far too much 'bad language,' there were too many violent oaths, and that the play itself was marred by this. I did not think it was fit to be put on the stage without cutting. It was agreed that it should be cut in rehearsal. A fortnight before its production Mr. Yeats, thinking I had seen a rehearsal, writes: 'I would like to know how you thought *The Playboy* acted. . . . Have they cleared many of the objectional sentences out of it?'

I did not, however, see a rehearsal and did not hear the play again until the night of its production, and then I told Synge that the cuts were not enough, that many more should be made. He gave me leave to do this, and in consultation with the players I took out many phrases which, though in the printed book, have never since that first production been spoken on our stage. I am sorry that they were not taken out before it had been played at all, but that is just what happened.

On Saturday, January 26th, 1907, I found a note from Synge on my arrival in Dublin: 'I do not know how things will go to-night. The day company are all very steady, but some of the outsiders in a most deplorable

state of uncertainty. . . . I have a sort of second edition of the influenza and I am looking gloomily at everything. Fay has worked very hard all through, and everything has gone smoothly.'

I think the week's rioting helped to break down his health. He was always nervous at a first production, and the unusual excitement of this one upset him and he took a chill and was kept to his bed for a while. Yet he got away to wild places while he could. He wrote to me from the Kerry coast:

'My journey went off all right, and though I had a terrible wet night in Tralee I was able to ride on here next day. When I came up to the house I found, to my horror, a large green tent pitched in the haggard and thought I had run my head into a Gaelic League settlement at last. However, it turned out to be a band of sappers only, who have since moved on.' And again: 'The day after to-morrow I move on, bag and baggage, to the Great Blasket Island. It is probably even more primitive than Aran, and I am wild with joy at the prospect. I will tell you of my new abode. I am to go out in a curragh[18] on Sunday, when the people are going back from Mass on the mainland, and I am to lodge with the King!'

It was only in the country places he was shy of the Gaelic League. In August, '06, he says: 'I went to the Oireactas on Thursday to see their plays. The propagandist play done by the Ballaghadereen Company was clever with some excellent dialogue, and the peasants who acted it were quite admirable. I felt really enthusiastic about the whole show, although the definitely propagandist fragments were, of course, very crude. The play was called, I think, *an T-Atruighe mor* (the big change). I think I have spelled it wrong. It would probably read badly.'

The last year was still a struggle against failing strength:—

'April, '08.—I have been waiting from day to day to write, so that I might say something definite about my "tin-tacks" (an allusion to the old man in *Workhouse Ward*[19] who has pains like tin-tacks in his inside) and possible plans. I was with the doctor again to-day, and he thinks I may have to go into hospital again, and perhaps have an operation, but things are uncertain for a day or two. . . . I fear there is little possibility of my being able to go to the shows this week, so I do not know if you ought to come up if you can without inconvenience. I am rather afraid of slovenly shows if there are poor houses and no one there to supervise. It is very trying having to drop my rehearsals of *Well of the Saints*[20]—in fact, this unlooked-for complication is a terrible upset every way—I have so much to do.'

'August 28th, '08.—I have just been with Sir E. Ball.[21] He seems to think I am going on very well, and says I may ride and bicycle and do what I like! All the same, I am not good for much yet. I get tired out very easily. I am half inclined to go to the British Association *matinée* on Friday. I would like to hear Yeats' speech, and I don't think it could do me any harm. In any case, I will go in and see you when you are up. I think of going away to Germany or somewhere before very long. I am not quite well enough for

the West of Ireland in this broken weather, and I think the complete change would do me most good. I have old friends on the Rhine I could stay with if I decide to go there. I hear great accounts of the Abbey this week, it almost looks as if Dublin was beginning to know we are there. I have been fiddling with my *Deirdre* a little. I think I'll have to cut it down to two longish acts. The middle act in Scotland is impossible. . . . They have been playing *The Well of the Saints* in Munich; I have just got £3 10s. royalties. It was a one-act version I have just heard this minute compressed from my text!'

'Jan. 3rd, '09.—I have done a great deal to *Deirdre* since I saw you, chiefly in the way of strengthening motives and re-casting the general scenario, but there is still a good deal to be done with the dialogue, and some scenes in the first act must be re-written to make them fit in with the new parts I have added. I only work a little every day, and I suffer more than I like with indigestion and general uneasiness inside. . . . The doctors are vague and don't say much that is definite. . . .

'They are working at *The Miser*[22] now, and are all very pleased with it and themselves. I have not been in to see a rehearsal yet, as I keep out in the country as much as I can.'

But his strength did not last long enough to enable him to finish *Deirdre of the Sorrows*,[23] his last play. After he had gone, we took infinite trouble to bring the versions together, and we produced it early in the next year, but it needed the writer's hand. I did my best for it, working at its production through snowy days and into winter nights, until rheumatism seized me with a grip I have never shaken off. I wrote to Mr. Yeats: 'I still hope we can start with *Deirdre*. . . . I will be in Dublin for rehearsals in Christmas week, though I still hope to get to Paris for Christmas with Robert,[24] but it may not be worth while. I will spend all January at the Theatre, but I must be back on the first of February to do some planting; that cannot be put off.' And again, 'I am more hopeful of *Deirdre* now. I have got Conchubar and Fergus off at the last in Deirdre's long speech, and that makes an immense improvement; she looks lonely and pathetic with the other two women crouching and rocking themselves on the floor.'

For we have done our utmost for his work since we lost him, as we did while he was with us here. He had written a poem, it was in the Scon-Eper Press at the time of his death:—

> 'With Fifteen-ninety or Sixteen-sixteen
> We end Cervantes, Marot, Nashe, or Green;
> Then Sixteen-thirteen till two score and nine
> Is Crashaw's niche, that honey-lipped divine.
> And so when all my little work is done,
> They'll say I came in Eighteen seventy-one,
> And died in Dublin—What year will they write
> For my poor passage to the stall of Night?'

Early in 1909 he was sent again into a private hospital in Dublin. A letter came to me from Mr. Yeats dated March 24th: 'In the early morning Synge said to the nurse, "It is no use fighting death any longer," and turned over and died.'

NOTES

For a note on Lady Gregory see p. 7.

1. At the time Synge visited Coole Park on 27 June 1898, Lady Gregory, who had become passionately concerned in Irish nationalism, was planning—with Edward Martyn and the already well-established George Moore and W. B. Yeats—the foundation of an Irish Literary Theatre, whose first production was to be Yeats's *The Countess Cathleen* and Martyn's *The Heather Field*. Synge visited Edward Martyn at Tullira Castle, five miles away from Coole in the company of Yeats, and took part in some of the discussions of the project.

2. *Cuchulain of Muirthemne* (London: Murray, 1902), a retelling of the stories from medieval Irish legend and saga centring upon the hero Cuchulain; was written in the Anglo-Irish dialect which later came to be known as Kiltartan, after a village in Galway near Coole Park. Synge reviewed the book in the *Speaker* in June 1902. Cuchlain (or Cuchulinn) is the champion hero of a cycle of Celtic myths who at the age of seventeen defended Ulster single-handed for four months.

3. For a note on Dr Douglas Hyde see p. 37.

4. Antonio Mancini (1852–1930), Italian genre portrait- and landscape-painter.

5. Rembrandt van Rijn (1606–69), Dutch painter and etcher.

6. Lady Gergory seems to be inaccurate here. Synge visited Coole for the first time in 1898. In 1900 he began writing his first play, *When the Moon Has Set*, which was rejected by Lady Gregory for the Irish Literary Theatre in 1901. In her account here she confused her recollections of Synge's first visit to Coole in 1898 with his second in 1901. Synge's first play is about a young Irish landlord who returns to Ireland from Paris and falls in love with a nun.

7. *The Shadow of the Glen* was first produced at the Molesworth Hall, Dublin, on 8 October 1903.

8. *Riders to the Sea* opened at the Molesworth Hall, Dublin, on 25 February 1904.

9. A. H. Bullen, the publisher.

10. For a note on John Masefield see p. 85.

11. Arthur Symons (1865–1945), one of the most influential men of letters in the last years of the nineteenth century. He was an expert on contemporary French literature, a member of the Rhymers' Club, and a regular contributor to the leading periodicals of the time. He collaborated with Aubrey Beardsley in producing *The Savoy* in 1896. His most important work is perhaps *The Symbolist Movement in Literature* (1899). He wrote many plays and books of poetry and published translations from six languages. He was a close friend of W. B. Yeats and was a supporter in the fight for the recognition of contemporary Irish writing.

12. *Samhain; An Occasional Review* (Dublin and London), edited for the Irish Literary Theatre by W. B. Yeats. Seven issues were published, October 1901 to November 1908.

13. Synge became a Director of the Irish National Theatre Society in 1905. His first experience could not have taken him through a more crucial period. He had difficulty keeping Yeats from feuding with AE [George Russell], who was in sympathy with the seceders. He helped the Fays to recruit and train new actors, and he continued to read new manuscripts submitted to the directors.

14. Fred M. Ryan, Secretary of the Irish National Theatre Society.

15. Lady Gregory's translation of Molière's *Le Médecin malgré lui* [The Physician in Spite of Himself, 1666] into Irish dialect. The play was produced at the Abbey Theatre on 16 April 1906.

16. Edward Millington Synge, who had a studio in the Boulevard Montparnasse while Synge was in Paris. The farmhouse Synge refers to was at Wintersells Farm, Byfleet, Surrey.

17. *The Shadowy Waters*, by W. B. Yeats, had its first production at the Abbey Theatre on 14 January 1904.

18. Light boat made of tarred canvas or leather stretched upon wooden ribs. During a visit to the island of Inishmaan, Synge's first ride in a curragh, the 'rude canvas canoe of a model that has served primitive races since men first went on the sea', gave him 'a moment of exquisite satisfaction'.

19. *The Workhouse Ward*, a comedy in one act by Lady Gregory, was first presented at the Abbey Theatre on 20 April 1908.

20. *The Well of the Saints*, by J. M. Synge, had its première at the Abbey Theatre on 4 February 1905. See previous memoir—William G. Fay, '*The Well of the Saints*', p. 30.

21. Sir Charles Ball, the surgeon who operated on Synge.

22. Lady Gregory's adaptation of Molière's *The Miser* opened at the Abbey Theatre on 21 January 1909.

23. *Deirdre of the Sorrows* was first produced at the Abbey Theatre on 13 January 1910.

24. Robert Gregory, Lady Gregory's son.

Synge*

GEORGE MOORE

And it was on one of those journeys[1] that he[2] discovered Synge, a man of such rough and uncultivated aspect that he looked as if he had come out of Derrinrush. He was not a peasant as Yeats first supposed, but came, like all great writers, from the middle classes; his mother had a house in Kingstown which he avoided as much as possible, and it was in the Rue d'Arras [sic] that Yeats found him, *dans une chambre meublée*[3] on the fifth floor. He was on his way back to Ireland, and might stay at Kingstown for a while, till his next quarter's allowance came in (he had but sixty pounds a year), but as soon as he got it he would be away to the West, to the Aran Islands. Yeats gasped; and it was the romance of living half one's life in the Latin Quarter and the other half in the Aran Islands that captured Yeats's imagination. He must have lent a willing ear to Synge's tale of an unpublished manuscript, a book which he had written about the Aran Islands;[4] but his interest in it doubtless flagged when Synge told him it was not written in peasant speech. Synge must have answered, 'But peasant speech in Aran is Irish.' Yeats remembered with regret that this was so, for he would have preferred Anglo-Irish; and he listened to Synge telling him that he had some colloquial knowledge of the Irish language. He had had to pick up a little Irish; life in Aran would be impossible without Irish, and Yeats awoke from his meditation.

This strange Irishman was a solitary, who only cared to talk with

* *English Review* (London) XVI (Feb 1914) 353–64, reprinted in *Vale* (London: William Heinemann, 1914) pp. 183–200.

peasants, and was interested in things rather than ideas. In the Rue d'Arras [d'Assas] it must have been Yeats that did all the admiration, and Synge must have been a little bored, but quite willing that Yeats should discover in him a man of genius, a strange experience for Synge, who, however convinced he was inly of his own genius, must have wondered how Yeats had divined it, for Yeats had not pretended to feel any interest in the articles on French writers that Synge had sent round to the English Press, adding thereby sometimes a few pounds to his income, but only sometimes, for these articles were so trite that they were seldom accepted; John Eglinton[5] confesses once a year that he could not stomach the article that Synge sent to him for publication in *Dana*;[6] and they were so incorrectly written that Best,[7] who knew Synge in the Rue d'Arras, tells that he used to go over them, for Synge could not write correctly at that time. Only one out of three was accepted, and the one that came to *Dana* no doubt came with all the edges worn by continual transmission through the post. It is Best that should write about Synge, for he helped him to furnish his room in the Rue d'Arras. Synge was very helpless in the actual affairs of life; he could not go out and buy furniture; Best had to go with him, and they brought home a mattress and some chairs and a bed on a barrow, and then returned to fetch the rest. There was a fiddle hanging on the wall of the garret in the Rue d'Arras, but as Synge never played it, Best began to wonder if Synge could play, and as if suspecting Best of disbelief in his music, Synge took it down one evening and drew the bow across the strings in a way that convinced Best, who played the fiddle himself; and, as if satisfied, he returned the fiddle to its nail, saying that he only played it in the Aran Islands in the evenings when the peasants wanted to dance. 'They have no ear for music,' he said, 'and do not recognise a melody.' 'What!' exclaimed Best. 'Well, only as they recognise the cry of a bird or animal, not as a musician.' 'Only the beat of the jig enters their ears,' Synge replied in a voice tinged with melancholy.

In Yeats's imagination playing the fiddle to the Aran Islanders, or reciting poems to them, is one and the same thing, and he recognised instantly in Synge the Gleeman that was in himself, but had remained, and would remain for ever, unrealised; and his imagination caught fire at the conjunction of the Rue d'Arras and the Aran Islands. 'Music coming to them in the springtime,' he may have murmured. It was easy to imagine that Synge could draw sweet music from the fiddle on the wall; for Yeats was at that time avid of music; he had lost his flute irreparably. . . . Synge would play new music for him, and he would beat the time, and it would be just the music that he wanted; his ears were weary of the three-holed Kiltartan whistle, and he forgot to ask himself if Lady Gregory would care for the richer music he was bringing back with him.

'Leave off writing articles on Anatole France, François Coppée, and Baudelaire, and come back to Ireland and write plays for me.'

Whosoever has followed this narrative so far can see Yeats leaning

forward in Synge's chair, getting more and more interested in him at every moment, his literary passions rising till they carried him to his feet and set him walking about the dusty carpet from the window to the table at which Synge worked, crying:

'You must make use of your Aran experiences.'

'But they are written; only no one will publish my book.'

'Your book is not written in the language of the peasant; I don't mean Irish, but Anglo-Irish, peasant idiom. You'll be able to translate from the Irish, and so thicken the idiom. Come to Ireland and write folk-plays for me. A play about Aran.'

'But the play I've shown you—'

'Is of no account. The language will help you to know your own people.'

And, better than any description, this dialogue represents the meeting of Yeats and Synge in the Rue d'Arras, Synge's large, impassive face into which hardly any light of expression ever came, listening to Yeats with a look of perplexity moving over its immobility, and Yeats's passion, purely literary, steadily mounting.

'You must come back and perfect yourself in the language. You must live among the people again,' he reports himself to have said. 'You must come to Ireland. A theatre is building in Dublin for the production of folk-plays.'

'Building!'

'Well, it will soon be building'; and he told Synge how Miss Horniman,[8] a lady of literary tastes and ample income, had decided to give to Dublin what no other city in an English-speaking country possessed—a subventioned theatre. 'Write me an Aran play. We will open the theatre with it'; and he began to speak of Synge's immediate return.

'As soon as the summer comes again.'

But that promise would not satisfy Yeats. Synge must return to Aran at once.

'I should die,' Synge is reported to have answered.

'Not before you have written the masterpiece,' was Yeats's answer, as related by himself; and Yeats continued day after day to subjugate Synge's mind, till one Saturday evening, after a talk lasting till long past midnight, Synge declared his adherence to the new creed.

'When a man's mind is made up, his feet must set out on the way.' Yeats's own words as reported by himself. He allowed, however, Synge to wait for two little cheques which he was owed for articles, and as soon as he received them he folded his luggage according to promise, and a few days after presented himself at the Nassau Hotel,[9] and was introduced to Lady Gregory, who, of course, perceived there was something on his mind. She encouraged him to confide in her, and he confided to her the story of his health, and she very kindly took his part against Yeats, who was all for Aran, not for the middle island, for there only Irish is spoken. 'And the dialect is what we want.'

'That may be, Mr. Yeats, but Mr. Synge may not be able to stand the climate in the autumn.' And she turned to Synge, who told her that the best time would be a little later, when the people would be digging in their potato-fields. Lady Gregory agreed that this was so, and after some demur Yeats yielded, as he always does to Lady Gregory, and the three were of one mind that the mild climate of Wicklow was most suitable for 'listening.'

'The tinkers meet there in the autumn.'

'You mustn't miss the gathering.'

He went away next morning, and his admirers were overjoyed when he wrote to them a few days afterwards saying that he had been fortunate enough to fall in with a band of tinkers driving their shaggy ponies, bony horses, and reliable asses up a hillside, making for their annual assemblage. They were exchanging their wives and arranging the roads they were to take, the signs to be left at the cross-roads, the fairs they were to attend, and the meeting-places for the following year. He had been very lucky, for he had fallen in with the tinkers at the moment when a tall, lean man turned to run after a screaming girl. 'Black Hell to your sowl! you've followed me so far, you'll follow me to the end!' he roared, seizing her by the wrist, a girl no doubt that had yielded to the call of the vagrant and had begun to regret her comfortable stead.

Without a trull, it is true, or the desire to win or to capture one, Synge, by his harmless appearance and his fiddle, gained the good-will of the tinker and his wife, and he followed the fortune of this family, listening to their talk as they strolled along the lanes, cadging and stealing as they went, squatting at eventide on the side of a dry ditch. Like a hare in a gap he listened, and when he had mastered every turn of their speech he left the tinker and turned into the hills, spending some weeks with a cottager, joining a little later another group of tinkers, accompanied by a servant-girl who had suddenly wearied of scrubbing and mangling, boiling for pigs, cooking, and working dough, and making beds in the evening. It would be better, she had thought, to lie under the hedgerow; and in telling me of this girl, Synge seemed to be telling me his own story. He, too, disliked the regular life of his mother's house, and preferred to wander with the tinkers, and when tired of them to lie abed smoking with a peasant, and awake amid the smells of shag and potato-skins in the sieve in the corner of the room. He told me how after breakfast he scrambled over a low wall out of which grew a single hawthorn, and looked round for a place where he might loosen his strap, and when that job was done he kept on walking ahead thinking out the dialogue of his plays, modifying it at every stile after a gossip with some herdsman or pig-jobber, whomever he might meet, returning through the cold spring evening, when the stars shine brightly through the naked trees, licking his lips, appreciating the fine flavour of some drunkard's oath or blasphemy.

He extended his tour through Connaught, spending a long time in my

own native town, Castlebar, where it is said he picked up no fewer than three or four turns of speech, and on his return to Dublin he had collected some hundreds in the different counties, and from different classes, and these he was able to work up together, creating what amounted practically to a small language understandable by everybody who knows English, but sufficiently far removed from ordinary speech to give his plays an air that none others have—that air of aloofness, of art, which Yeats deems necessary, which we all deem necessary, though we differ as to how it may be obtained. Synge had done what none had done before—he had discovered that it was possible to write beautifully in peasant idiom. Everybody could write it, Lady Gregory as well as another, but no one but Synge could write beautifully in it.

Yeats was at this time in the hands of the Fays[10] and a Committee, and the performances of the National Theatre were given in different halls; and when Synge came up from the country to read *Riders to the Sea* to the company, Yeats, who did not wish to have any misunderstanding on the subject, cried 'Sophocles' across the table, and, fearing that he was not impressive enough, he said: 'No, Æschylus.' And that same afternoon he said to me in Grafton Street: 'I would I were as sure of your future and of my own as I am of Synge's.' One of those exaggerated appreciations that annoy and estrange, and when I heard this one-act play, it seemed very little more than the contents of Synge's notebook, an experiment in language rather than a work of art, a preparatory essay; he seemed to me to have contented himself with relating a painful rather than a dramatic story, his preoccupation being to discover a style, a vehicle of expression, and it was not until Synge wrote *The Well of the Saints* that I began to feel that a man of genius had been born unto Ireland.

Irishmen had written well before Synge, but they had written well by casting off Ireland; but here was a man inspired by Ireland, a country that had not inspired any art since the tenth or twelfth century, a country to which it was fatal to return. Was Synge the exception, and was he going to find his fortune in Ireland? His literary fortune, for *The Well of the Saints* emptied the Abbey Theatre. It had never been full, the audiences were scanty, the patrons of the stalls being the Yeats family, Sarah Purser,[11] William Bailey,[12] John Eglinton, Æ,[13] Longworth,[14] and dear Edward,[15] who supported the Abbey Theatre, believing himself in duty bound to do so. He was averse from peasant plays, and *The Well of the Saints* upset him altogether. 'All this sneering at Catholic practices is utterly distasteful to me. Don't think I don't see it. I understand it very well, and I can hear it all, and the whining voice of the proselytiser. I never will go against my opinions. When I hear the Sacred Name I assure you—'

'You mean the name of God, Edward, don't you?'

'I never like to mention it. The Sacred Name is sufficient.'

'But if you are speaking French you say "Mon Dieu!" at every sentence, and what isn't wrong in one language, can't be wrong in another.'

A smile trickled across Edward's face, round and large and russet as a ripe pumpkin, and he muttered: '*Mon ami Moore, mon ami Moore.*'

He was in the Abbey the first night of *The Playboy*, and on my return from Paris he told me that, though the noise was great, he had heard enough blasphemy to keep him out of the theatre from thenceforth, and next morning he had read in the papers that Ireland had been exhibited in a shameful light as an immoral country.

'And oddly enough, the scene of the immorality is your own native town, George.'

He told me that the hooting had begun about the middle of the third act at the words: 'If all the women of Mayo were standing before me, and they in their—' He shrank from completing the sentence, and muttered something about the evocation of a disgusting spectacle.

'I agree with you, Edward, that shift evokes a picture of blay calico; but the delightful underwear of Madame ——'

'Now, George.'

And then, amused at his own folly, which he can no more overcome than anybody else, he began to laugh, shaking like a jelly, puffing solemnly all the while at his church-warden.

'The indignation was so great that I thought sometimes the pit was going to break in. "Lower the bloody curtain, and give us something we bloody well want," a well-filled pit kept on shouting.' And looking at Edward I imagined I could see him in the stalls near the stage, turning round in terror, his face growing purpler and purpler. 'All the same,' he said, 'though the pain that Synge's irreverent remarks caused me is very great, I disapprove altogether of interrupting a performance. But Yeats shouldn't have called in the police. A Nationalist should never call for the police.'

'But, Edward, supposing a housebreaker forces his way in here or into Tillyra?' [*sic*][16]

He said that that was different, and after wasting some time in discussion regarding the liberty of speech and the rights of property, he asked me if I had read the play, and I told him that on reading about the tumult in the Abbey Theatre I had telegraphed from Paris for a copy, and that the first lines convinced me that Ireland had at last begotten a masterpiece—the first lines of Pegeen Mike's letter to Mr. Michael O'Flaherty, general dealer, in Castlebar, for six yards of stuff for to make a yellow gown, a pair of boots with lengthy heels on them and brassy eyes, a hat is suited for a wedding day, a fine-tooth comb. 'Never was there such a picture of peasant life in a few lines'; and at every sentence my admiration increased. At the end of the act I cried out: 'A masterpiece! a masterpiece! of course, they were insulted.' The girls coming in with presents for the young stranger pleased me, but a cold wind of doubt seemed to blow over the pages when the father came on the stage, a bloody bandage about his head, and—

'Edward—you're asleep!'

'No, I'm listening.'

'So clearly did I see disaster in that bloody bandage that I could hardly read through the third act. But you see nothing in the play.'

'Yes, I do, only it's a little thing. Shawn Keogh is a very good character, and the Widow Quinn is not bad either.'

'But the language, Edward.'

'You have made up your mind that this play is a masterpiece, but I am not going to give in to you.'

'But the style, Edward.'

'It isn't English. I like the Irish language and the English language, but I don't like the mixture'; and then puffing at his pipe for a few seconds he said, 'I like the intellectual drama.'

The conversation turned upon Ibsen, and we talked pleasantly until one in the morning, and then bidding him good-night I returned to Ely Place, delighted at my own perspicacity, for there could be no doubt that it was the bloody bandage that caused the row in the Abbey Theatre.

'The author and Yeats expect too much from the audience; the language is beautiful, but—' I had admitted to Edward that I had only glanced through the third act, and Edward had answered, 'If you had read the whole of it you might be of my opinion.' It wasn't likely that Edward and I should agree about the *Playboy*, but it might well be that I was judging it hurriedly, and it would have been wiser, I reflected, to have read the play through before attempting to explain why the humour of the audience had changed suddenly, and I resolved to read the play next morning. But my dislike of reading is so great that I missed it, and when Yeats came to see me, instead of the praise which he had come to hear, and which he was craving for, he heard some rather vain dissertations and only half-hearted praise. Again my impulsiveness was my ruin. The play would have been understood if it had been read carefully, and the evening would have been one of exaltation, whereas it went by mournfully, Yeats in the chimney-corner listening to suggestions that would preserve the comedy note. He went away depressed, saying, however, that it would be as well that I should write to Synge about his play, since I liked the greater part. But he did not think that Synge would make any alterations.[17] And the letter I sent to Synge was superficial. I hope he destroyed it. He was glad that his play had pleased me, but he could not alter the third act. It had been written again and again—thirteen times. That is all I remember of his letter, interesting on account of the circumstances in which it was written and the rarity of Synge's correspondence. It is a pity his letter was destroyed and no copy kept; our letters would illuminate the page that I am now writing, exhibiting us both in our weakness and our strength—Synge in his strength, for if the play had been altered we should have all been disgraced, and it was Yeats's courage that saved us in Dublin. He did not argue, he piled affirmation upon affirmation, and he succeeded in the end . . . but we will not anticipate.

But if Dublin would not listen to the *Playboy,* Dublin read the text; edition after edition was published, and we talked the *Playboy* round our firesides. How we talked! Week after week, month after month, the Abbey Theatre declining all the while, till at last the brothers Fay rose in revolt against Yeats's management, accusing him of hindering the dramatic movement by producing no plays except those written by his intimate friends. Yeats repelled the accusation by offering to submit those that he had rejected to the judgment of Professor Tyrrell, a quite unnecessary concession on the part of Yeats, for Willie Fay is but an amusing Irish comedian, and it was presumptuous for him and his brother to set themselves against a poet. They resigned, and one night Yeats came to me with the grave news that the Fays had seceded.

'I feel I must talk to somebody,' he said, flinging himself into a chair.

Æ is the only man who can distribute courage, but Yeats and Æ were no longer friends, and I was but a poor purveyor. It is true that I told him, and without hesitation, that the secession of the Fays was a blessing in disguise, and that now he was master in his own house the Abbey Theatre would begin to flourish, and it would have been well if I had confined myself to pleasant prophesying; but very few can resist the temptation to give good advice.

'One thing, Yeats, I have always had in mind, but never liked to tell you; it is that the way you come down the steps from the stage and stride up the stalls and alight by Lady Gregory irritates the audience, and if you will allow me to be perfectly frank, I will tell you that she is a little too imposing, too suggestive of Corinne or Madame de Stael.[18] Corinne and Madame de Stael were one and the same person, weren't they? But you don't know, Yeats, do you?'

And so I went on pulling the cord, letting down volumes of water upon poor Yeats, who crouched and shivered. The water, always cold, was at times very icy, for instance when I said that his dreams of reviving Jonson's *Volpone* must be abandoned.

'If you aren't very careful, Yeats, the Academic idea will overgrow the folk.' And Yeats went away overwhelmed, and I saw no more of him for many months, not until it became known that Synge's persistent ill-health had at last brought him to a private hospital, where he lay waiting an operation. 'He lives by the surgeon's knife,' Yeats said to me, and I welcomed his advice to save myself from the anguish of going to see a man dying of cancer. And while Synge perished slowly, Gogarty[19] recovered in the same hospital after an operation for appendicitis. One man's scale drops while another's goes up. As I write this line I can see Synge, whom I shall never see again with my physical eyes, sitting thick and straight in my armchair, his large, uncouth head, and flat, ashen-coloured face with two brown eyes looking at me, not unsympathetically. A thick, stubbly growth of hair starts out of a strip of forehead like black twigs out of the head of a broom. I see a ragged moustache, and he sits bolt upright in my chair, his

legs crossed, his great country shoe spreading over the carpet. The conversation about us is of literature, but he looks as bored as Jack Yeats does in the National Gallery. . . . Synge and Jack Yeats are like each other in this, neither takes the slightest interest in anything except life, and in their own deductions from life; educated men, both of them, but without aesthetics, and Yeats's stories that Synge read the classics and was a close student of Racine [20] is a piece of Yeats's own academic mind. Synge did not read Racine oftener than Jack Yeats looks at Titian, [21] and no conclusion should be drawn from the fact that among his scraps of verse are to be found translations from Villon [22] and Marot; [23] they are merely exercises in versification; he was curious to see if Anglo-Irish idiom could be used in poetry; Villon wrote largely in the slang of his time, therefore Villon was selected; and whosoever reads Villon dips into Marot and reads *Une ballade à double refrain*. And that is all, for, despite his beautiful name, Marot is an insipid poet. I am sorry that Yeats fell into the mistake of attributing much reading to Synge; he has little love of character and could not keep himself from putting rouge on Synge's face and touching up his eyebrows. He showed greater discrimination when he said, 'You will never know as much about French poetry as Arthur Symons. Come to Ireland and write plays for me.' And for his great instinct we must forgive him his little sins of reason. He very rightly speaks of Synge as a solitary, and it is interesting to speculate what made him a solitary. Was it the sense that death was lurking round the corner always, and the sense that he possessed no social gifts that helped to drive him out into the Aran Islands, where he knew nobody, and to the Latin Quarter behind the Luxembourg Gardens, where nobody knew him? A man soon perceives if he be interested in others and if others be interested in him, and if he contribute nothing and get nothing, he will slink away as Synge did.

Yeats had called him out of obscurity for a little while, and now he was to pass from us into the night that never melts into dawn, unless glory be the dead man's dawn. It seemed a cruel fate that decreed that Synge must die before his play could be revived in Dublin, but his fate was cruel from the beginning. Yeats tells me that these lines were found among his papers: 'I am five-and-twenty to-day; I wonder will the five-and-twenty years before me be as unhappy as those I have passed through.' And well might he have doubted that his middle life would be less unpleasant. He received Yeats's belief in his genius, and that was all. He wrote but little, but that little was his own: *Mon verre est petit mais je bois dans mon verre*.[24] His last strength he reserved for *Deirdre*, working at the play whenever he could, determined to finish it before he died. But he wrote slowly, and the disease moved quickly from cell to cell, and before the last writing was accomplished Synge laid aside the pen and resigned himself to death. It is curious that he should have met his old friend Best on his way to the hospital. Best tells these things significantly. He asked Synge if he were going in for an operation. Synge answered no; and when Best called to see him in the hospital, he found

Synge clinging to a little hope, though he knew there was none, saying that people often got better when nobody expected them to get better; and he seemed to experience some disappointment when Best did not answer promptly that that was so.

He used to speak of *Deirdre* as his last disappointment; but another awaited him. An hour before he died he asked the nurse to wheel his bed into a room whence he could see the Wicklow mountains, the hills where he used to go for long solitary walks, and he was wheeled into the room, but the mountains could not be seen from the windows; to see them it was necessary to stand up, and Synge could not stand or sit up in his bed, so his last wish remained ungratified, and he died with tears in his eyes.

NOTES

George Moore (1852–1933), Irish novelist and man of letters. As an innovator in fiction he does not now seem so important as he once did, but *Esther Waters* (1894) will always deserve readers, and in an autobiographical trilogy, *Hail and Farewell* (1911–14), he gained the rare achievement of finding an original prose form of his own outside the novel. In Paris Moore became friendly with the *avant-garde* Impressionist group vividly described in *Reminiscences of the Impressionist Painters* (1906). Another account of the years in Paris, in which he introduced the younger generation in England to his version of *fin-de-siècle* decadence, was his first autobiography *Confessions of a Young Man* (1888). Moore moved to Dublin, where he contributed notably to the planning of the Irish Literary Theatre, but Irish politics and clericalism sent him back to England in 1911. While he lived in Dublin he produced a volume of fine short stories about Ireland, *The Untilled Field* (1903) and an experimental novel, *The Lake* (1905), where he developed the 'melodic line'.

1. To Paris.
2. W. B. Yeats.
3. In a furnished room.
4. Yeats and Lady Gregory had tried to have *The Aran Islands* published, and John Quinn of New York had offered to pay the expense of making plates for it, but Yeats had said he wanted the book taken on its merits, even if Synge had to wait years for a publisher.
5. John Eglinton [William Kirkpatrick Magee] (1868–1961), Irish essayist and poet. A school friend of W. B. Yeats, he appears in James Joyce's *Ulysses*. His works include *Two Essays on the Remnant* (1896), *Pebbles from a Brook* (1901), *Bards and Saints* (1906), *Anglo-Irish Essays* (1917), *Irish Literary Portraits* (1935), *A Memoir of A.E.* (1937) and *Confidential; or Take It or Leave It* (1951).
6. *Dana; A Magazine of Independent Thought* (Dublin), ed. by John Eglinton and Frederick Ryan. May 1904—April 1905, twelve issues in all.
7. For a note on Dr Richard Best see p. 47.
8. For a note on Miss Horniman see p. 29.
9. In Dublin.
10. For a note on the Fays see p. 29.
11. Sarah Purser (1848–1943), Irish artist who founded a co-operative society of artists known as An Tur Gloine [The Tower of Glass] in 1902. The stained-glass windows in the vestibule of the old Abbey Theatre were designed by her. She was a friend of the Yeats family. See Elizabeth Coxhead, 'Sarah Purser and the Tower of Glass', *Daughters of Erin* (London: Secker and Warburg, 1965) pp. 125–66.
12. Sir William Henry Bailey (1894–1913), Chairman and Managing Director, W. H. Bailey and Co.; President, Library Association of the United Kingdom 1906–7; and President of the Manchester Arts Club and of the Manchester Shakespeare Society.

13. For a note on AE [George Russell] see p. 47.
14. Francis Longworth (1834–1898), H.M. Lord-Lieutenant and Custos Rotulorum for County Westmeath from 1892. Moore is surely wrong here since the Abbey Theatre began in 1904, six years after Longworth's death.
15. Edward Martyn (1859–1923), who, by financial support and his two best plays *The Heather Field* (1899) and *Maeve* (1900), did much to set the Irish Dramatic Movement on its feet. It was in 1899 that W. B. Yeats, Edward Martyn, George Moore and Lady Gregory founded the Irish Literary Theatre in Dublin under the auspices of the National Literary Society created in 1891. See Sister Marie-Therese Courtney, *Edward Martyn and the Irish Theatre* (New York: Vantage Press, 1956).
16. Tullira Castle, Edward Martyn's country residence, five miles away from Coole.
17. In the third act, after Old Mahon and Christy meet face to face, the whole play alters its perspective, and characters once found endearing are found to be ignorant, vicious and treacherous. Moore recognized this shift in the play when he wanted Synge to alter the ending, saying, 'Your end is not comedy, it ends on a disagreeable note.' He found the physical violence at the end most unacceptable.
18. Anne-Louise-Germaine de Staël (1766–1817), French prose-writer. The only child of the financier Necker, later to be so famous in the events leading to the French Revolution, her mother having once been the object of the historian Edward Gibbon's love, she was given an unusually full education for girls of the day and was busy with her pen before she was twenty. Her writings include *Réflexions sur le procès de la Reine* (1793), *Littérature et ses rapports avec les institutions sociales* (1800), *Delphine* (1802), *Corinne* (1805), *Considération sur la révolution française* (1818) and the autobiographical *Dix and d'exil* (1821).
19. For a note on Oliver St John Gogarty see p. 35.
20. Jean-Baptiste Racine (1639–99), French dramatic poet who was a member of a group including La Fontaine, Boileau and Molière. His plays include *Andromaque* (1667), *Britannicus* (1669), *Bérénice* (1670), *Bajazet* (1672), *Mithridate* (1673), *Iphigénie* (1674) and *Phèdre* (1677). When W. B. Yeats first met Synge in Paris, Synge was planning a critical work on Racine—then and always one of his favourite writers—and had just been reading Corneille. 'Give up Paris,' Yeats said to Synge, 'You will never create anything by reading Racine, and Arthur Symons will always be a better critic of French literature.'—Introduction to *The Well of the Saints*.
21. Titian (1477–1576), Italian painter.
22. François Villon (1431(?)–66(?)), French poet who is regarded as the first and one of the greatest of French lyricists.
23. Clement Marot (1495(?)–1544), French poet who as a graceful satirist had few equals in the whole range of French literature, and who is the link between French medieval and modern poetry.
24. My glass is small, but I drink from my own glass.

Synge and the Irish*

JOHN B. YEATS

The acrimonious dispute carried on in the newspapers over John M. Synge and his plays is the eternal dispute between the man of prose and the man of imagination. Synge's plays, his prefaces to his plays, and his book on the Aran Islands, like his conversation, describe a little community rich in natural poetry, in fancy, in wild humor, and in wild philosophy; as wild flowers among rocks, these qualities spring out of their lives of incessant danger and incessant leisure; there are also bitter herbs. When I used to listen to Synge's conversation, so rare and sudden, as now when I read or listen to what he has written, I can say to myself, 'Here among these peasants is the one spot in the British Islands, the one spot among English-speaking people, where Shakespeare would have found himself a happy guest.'

* * *

Synge's history was peculiar. He took up music as his profession and studied it in Germany, Rome, and Paris; and having only a very small income, for economy's sake always lived with poor people. In Paris he stayed with a man cook and his wife, who was a *couturière*. He told me that they had but one sitting-room, in which the man did his cooking and the wife her sewing, with another sewing-woman who helped. When, as sometimes happened, a large order for hats came in, Synge, who by this time had given up music for philology, would drop his studies and apply himself also to hat-making, bending wires, etc. After a year or so he moved into a hotel, where he met my son,[1] who urged him to leave Paris for the west of Ireland and apply himself to the study of Irish. Among these western peasants he thenceforth spent a great part of every winter, living as one of the family, they calling one another by their Christian names; and he told me that he would rather live among them than in the best hotel.

Synge was morally one of the most fastidious men I ever met, at once too sensitive and too proud and passionate ever to stoop for a moment to any kind of action that would be unworthy. He was a well-built, muscular man, with broad shoulders, carrying his head finely. He had large, light-hazel eyes which looked straight at you. His conversation, like his book on

---

* Extracted from *Harper's Weekly* (New York) LV (25 Nov 1911) 17, reprinted in *Essays Irish and American* (Dublin: Talbot Press; London: T. Fisher Unwin, 1918) pp. 51–61.

the Aran Islands, had the charm of absolute sincerity, a quality rare among men and artists, though it be the one without which nothing else matters. He neither deceived himself nor anybody else, and yet he had the enthusiasm of the poet. In this combination of enthusiasm and veracity he was like that other great Irishman, Michael Davitt.[2] Like Davitt, also, he was without any desire to be pugnacious: resolute, yet essentially gentle, he was a man of peace.

NOTES

John Butler Yeats (1839–1922), W. B. Yeats's father, a distinguished artist and a member of the Royal Hibernian Academy. Synge's *In the Shadow of the Glen* was praised by John Butler Yeats for its attack upon 'our Irish institution, the loveless marriage'. In 1905 John Butler Yeats was commissioned to make a portrait of Synge for the Dublin Municipal Gallery. W. B. Yeats described this portrait in a notable poem:

> And here's John Synge himself, that rooted man,
> 'Forgetting human words,' a grave deep face.

1. W. B. Yeats.
2. Michael Davitt (1846–1906), Irish Nationalist leader and founder of the Irish Land League (1879); author of *Leaves from a Prison Diary* (1884) and *The Fall of Feudalism in Ireland* (1904).

I Remember J. M. Synge*

JAMES STEPHENS

It was not until late in his rather short life that Synge discovered his true ability to lie neither in philosophy nor music but in drama, and one may wonder how he came to make this discovery, for he was a painfully slow writer, and his very slowness might have led him to distrust an art-form that was so difficult to handle. To the end writing was a toil to him.

In this, however, he was not exceptional; for the majority of writers have assured us that writing is a labour from which one may really shrink a little. Synge occasionally got some reviewing to do for a literary weekly, but he had to discontinue this because the article, for which he might receive two guineas, always cost him six weeks to write; and these were six weeks of painful cogitation as to how possibly one can say anything whatever with a pen that will afterwards be readable.

* Broadcast on BBC on Thursday, 15 March 1928, reprinted in *Radio Times* (London) (23 Mar 1928) pp. 590, 611 and as 'Reminiscences of J. M. Synge', *James, Seumas & Jacques. Unpublished Writings of James Stephens,* chosen and edited with an introduction by Lloyd Frankenberg (London: Macmillan, 1964) pp. 54–60.

Still later he confessed that if his day's work had actually resulted in the addition of two words to his manuscript, although he might not feel triumphant and inclined to celebrate the occasion, he did yet consider that the day had not been wasted, that his subject had been carried on, or was not absolutely stationary.

He lived in Paris for some years at the rue d'Assas, and his apartment was adequately furnished with a bed, an oil-stove, a book-case, and a yard of French bread, and while in Paris he really needed whatever scarce guineas might come his way. Possibly the philosophy he toiled after was sufficiently robust at this time to tide him over the bad days but, although he did not complain, he did consider that a meal which cost more than one franc twenty-five had been extravagantly paid for.

He was somewhat negative to ordinary human beings (the dramatist tends to be so), not that he disliked people, but he did not admire them. He certainly did not love his fellow-human-beings in the mass. With him more than six people could easily become a crowd, and he could consider that such a gathering would have neither wit nor looks. The dramatist will love the rare, the personal, the individual, but he cannot even be expected to love the multitude.

Dramatic qualities were to Synge more easily discoverable in the countryside than in the city. He thought that every country-bread person has a measurable idiosyncrasy: has each a distinct nose and hat and accent.

And in the country he found many another cherishable thing. Birds and beasts and plants are there. There the earth itself seems to be more manifest. Each rod of it is there observed to be utterly different from any other possible rod of space. Every slope and ridge and hill; every stream and tree and cloud is known as distint from every other similar sight or bulk in the world.

A moor (or, as we should say in Ireland, a bog) was not for Synge a place from which turf or peat is cut. A bog was an enchantment, as indeed it is to everyone who has become acquainted with or has lived nigh to a bog. To get well into an extensive bog is to leave all else behind; is to have left the world behind; almost to have left one's self afar and apart and forgotten. There is the bog and the clouds, and the rest merges to them.

The sea is desolate, but it is also, and unforgivably, a desolation; but the bog is not a desolation; it is desolate, but is habitable and inhabited. Birds and rats and bees and rabbits are there. An odd donkey or a goat is always, somewhere, ambling or frisking away from you; is always cropping an endless breakfast. For in a bog you could easily imagine that the breakfast of a donkey began before time began, and that it will continue while time has yet a second to draw on.

And over it all there is wind and space and cloud and silence; the wind always different, and the cloud never the same, the silence never monotonous. All these seem to live as it were one life, and one's own life participates into that, or seems scarcely to be sundered from it.

He loved some other matters also; that is, his mind went willingly to certain things. He loved music and occultism and a something that we shall call bleakness. Whatever might be authoritatively uttered on these subjects would be diligently hearkened to by him.

Music, where it is understood, is loved by most of us, for we may only love where we understand. Occultism, or the theory of magic, is delighted in by everyone who is sane enough to wish to be saner; to wish, that is, to be wiser. But bleakness is another thing, and touches only to the fine soul. It is the especial, perhaps the final, acquirement of a cultured person. At last nothing but it is beauty. That is, nothing but bleakness can definitely satisfy the true man that is in every man.

Had he lived longer Synge might have carved a bare, an unadorned, a lean bleak art to replace the lush and somewhat vociferous art that he has left us. His art is lush, but there is continually to be found in it the wiry line, the rigour, the sharp and bare and bleak that he truly loved, and which he would have further striven to.

His knowledge of the countryside was extensive and penetrating. He knew the call of every bird and the habit of most creatures that are to be found in our ways and pastures. His approach to knowledge was—to be silent; to look eagerly at all that came; and to listen intently to all that happened. And, in his approach to a knowledge of the human inhabitants of the countryside, he used the same approach and attitude.

As a boy he had wandered the hills of Dublin and Wicklow, and he knew these intimately. He could assure a thirsty companion that behind a certain folding of a certain hilly track there was a well. And, if one was thirstier still, he would tell behind how many hills-and-a-half a tavern lay: or that on sixteen rising turns to the left a slaty cottage was couched among slaty rocks and that there one could get a glass of milk and a cake from the griddle.

And he knew that in all these places, if one were well-bred—if, that is, one were silent and inconspicuous—there could be heard a fashion of speech which was not conned from books; which had no acquaintance with art or science or scholarship, and which was yet abundant and racy and of a remarkable texture—the wild, the exuberant speech of isolated people. People who are always as timid in action as they are bold in talk: being bold indeed in the only thing they have practice of. For from these people every adventure but the adventure of speech has been retired, and they must seek in conversation all of the change, all of the excitement that others win from travel, from theatres, from the press of men and affairs.

He was different from many of his countrymen in a number of ways. One, but of prime importance, was that he came of a Protestant stock. A stock that included bishops and canons and missionaries who, through generations, had been to and returned from distant lands and curious peoples. He grew in a house that was filled with the furnitures and curiosities of strange countries.

His true schooling was up in the mountain and out on the bog; it came from the shy but vital life that moves in solitudes. His professors were the mountainy men and women, themselves almost as humble in station, almost as sundered from change, almost as bereft of ambition, but as vital, persistent, self-centred as was the lowly animal life that throve about them.

From these teachers he learned to delight in the curious cadences that may be in speech. He learned the craft of packing a phrase until it is explosive with adventure; the art of lightening however tragic or despairing a concept with just the irony or humour or tenderness that brings it back to earth and to a human relation.

He loved the village tailor who said, 'I will make you a suit, sir, that will go around and about you like a curtain.'

And when he once lamented the ageing condition of his own hat he was comforted by the remark of the person to whom he was speaking:—'Let you not throw away the hat,' quoth his companion, 'for there is an art about an old hat that is not in a new hat.'

And what might that art be? Synge enquired.

'The art of an old hat is to cock it, and 'tis known that no person whatever would care to cock a new hat.'

He loved the simple human relation, and however fantastic a tale he may be telling, it is always human. Perhaps his limitation lay here. He is a folk-writer working on folk material. His fantasy does not attempt anything but the world we live in; does not bid for an extra world or a spiritual experience. His tales are wonderful indeed; but they are wonderful because of the bog and the mountain that are in them; because of the men and women that rage and riot in them; because of all the things that he knew and loved so well.

And in this he differs from the other writers of his quality. The quest after divinity that is the Irish writer's torment and his joy, brought to Synge neither joy nor torment. Perhaps he had no time for these. 'Men and women and their delicious burdens' were what he sought and wrote of. The common physical and mental vigour of life was what he loved and would seek. He was for years a sick man, and perhaps guessing that he was a doomed man, he did not search for another world, and a greater being: divining that he must quit the habitual earth, the companionable sun, the comforting spaces ere he could really fathom these or savour this life to the full.

A silent, an aloof, a listening man! Listening to and watching all that which had never been completely his, and from which he should soon be parted. He would stand on a headland that jutted steeply on the sea, and he would look and look and look at the sparkling waters below. He would look at a meadow, a sunset, a man, as though he must satiate his eyes with their wonder, and, if it could be, saturate his very being with all that he should not carry with him.

He died in a Dublin hospital. A doctor who attended him told that when

his end was nigh, Synge petitioned that he might be lifted in bed so that he should look from the window and see the Dublin hills. Twice he was so lifted, and he looked again on the shapes that he loved better than all other shapes of the world.

But when on the third morning he looked from the window, he looked on blankness; there was a thick mist without, and he could not see the hills. As he was lowered again he was weeping, quietly, forlornly, and in a little time he died.

NOTE

James Stephens (1882–1950), Irish poet and novelist. His poetry collections include *Insurrections* (1909), *The Hill of Vision* (1912) and *Reincarnation* (1918). Among his other works are *The Charwoman's Daughter* (1912), *The Crock of Gold* (1912), *Here Are Ladies* (1913), *The Demi-Gods* (1914), *The Rockey Road to Dublin* (1915), *Songs from the Clay* (1915), *Deirdre* (1923), *In the Land of Youth* (1924), *Etched in Moonlight* (1928) and *Kings and the Moon* (1938). Almost all these books, except *The Crock of Gold*, are out of print. But his eye-witness account of the Easter Rising, *The Insurrection in Dublin*, was reprinted in 1965. See Birgit Bramsback, *James Stephens; A Literary and Bibliographical Study* (Cambridge, Massachusetts: Harvard University Press, 1959); Hilary Pyle, *James Stephens; His Work and An Account of His Life* (London: Routledge and Kegan Paul, 1965); and *The Letters of James Stephens*, ed. Richard Finneran (London: Macmillan, 1974).

J. M. Synge*

W. R. RODGERS (*editor*)

And so when all my little work is done
They'll say I came in eighteen-seventy-one.[1]

In April of that year John Synge was born of respectable and godly parents, near Dublin. He was barely twelve months old when his father died. Years later, Seamus O'Sullivan called to see him at his mother's house in Kingstown where he was living.

SEAMUS O'SULLIVAN:[2] I was shown into a large room in which Synge was seated at a table strewn with yellow-covered French books, but the walls of the room in which he sat were covered from floor to ceiling by volumes of theological works. As I looked from these to the paper-covered books, which obviously occupied the dramatist, I remembered suddenly that Synge was the descendant of a long line of Church of Ireland dignitories, amongst them Edward, Bishop of Elphin, who so wisely rejected that gaudily dressed young probationer, Oliver Goldsmith, and by so doing

* Broadcast on BBC in May 1952, reprinted in *Irish Literary Portraits* (London: British Broadcasting Corporation, 1972) pp. 94–115.

saved the Church from the acquisition of a very half-hearted clergyman—and the world from the loss of a great poet.

Too many books spoil the cloth. But, from the narrow school of family catechists the poet in John Synge escaped, quickly, into the wordless air and bookless wilds of the Dublin hills. As a boy he says,

> I knew the stars, the flowers, and the birds,
> The grey and wintry sides of many glens,
> And did but half remember human words
> In converse with the mountains, moors, and fens.

He was a solitary, silent, meditative lad not greatly given to reading, says Edward Millington Stephens, his nephew—

EDWARD MILLINGTON STEPHENS:[3] He was always a naturalist, greatly taken by books on natural history.[4] As a boy he suffered considerably from colds in the head and rather tended to asthma, so he didn't attend school very regularly. I don't think his mother thought it mattered very much. He did go to school for a while, then he had a tutor, before he entered Trinity College. But he seems to have read, by himself, a lot of things other boys mightn't have done. At about fourteen he read Darwin's *Origin of Species,*[5] and that upset his faith, because he was accustomed to a doctrine which regards the Bible as infallible from cover to cover and the Garden of Eden as just as important as any other part of it.

> If Church and State reply
> Give Church and State the lie.

John Synge would often quote these lines in later years. But as a lad, his shy defection from the faith grieved his mother and troubled himself.

STEPHENS: I always regard his mother as a great influence on his life. She was one of the old school—she brought up all her children very thoroughly instructed in what you might call the evangelical protestant faith—actually her father came from the north, from Antrim, and her mother from Starbane, so she really had a northern tradition. Her father died in the potato famine. He was a clergyman in County Cork.

She was one of that downright, upright, Northern breed which loves a good floury potato and a good flowery sermon. A great expositor of the Bible.

STEPHENS: She certainly was. She had a marvellous gift, and not only did she instruct her own children, but she instructed her grandchildren, so that I know exactly the same teaching as John got as a child. He looked on her really as an example of what a woman ought to be.

So much so, that when he first fell in love it was with a young woman[6] *of strong religious conviction.*

STEPHENS: She was an early attachment. It was an attachment he referred to as an imaginative devotion, really, to a lady who didn't share his opinions or his ambitions. She was a pleasant girl, who lived in the same terrace as his mother and had once been his mother's guest for a part of the summer holiday in County Wicklow. She liked country life and used to sketch in water-colours and read Wordsworth; and of course she liked John's attentions.

But, though they met often on the road, they had very few opportunities of spending any time together. Her father was a leader among the Plymouth Brethren, and she accepted altogether his evangelical teaching. She would never have thought of marrying a man who, though strict and ascetic in his mode of life, could not agree with her doctrinal beliefs about salvation.

All the same, Synge's puritan upbringing put its mark on him permanently. His frugal way of life, for instance '£40 a year and a new suit when I am too shabby.' His sober reticence. His stubborn single-mindedness. His rigid regard for the truth, for the exact and living phrase.

STEPHENS: I regard him as having been just the same to the end. He was an ascetic person who was very strict in his behaviour in every way, and he hated anything in the way of a lie. I remember one day my brother and I were going out—I was carrying a rook-rifle and my brother was carrying a gun—and he said we mustn't go each with firearms or we'd shoot each other. So I said we wouldn't load them both at the same time. We didn't, until we got to a place where we were stalking a rabbit and the rabbit was sitting up and I loaded my rifle to have a shot at it. I told him about this when I came back, not regarding it as any violation of my promise because I wasn't carrying the rifle loaded, but he gave me a tremendous lecture on speaking the truth.

Out of Synge's sober code of behaviour came the playboy, by reaction.

STEPHENS: In 1902—it was the year that his plays really came to fruition—my brother and I had a bedroom off his, and he was very pleasant with boys—we could take liberties with him that you mightn't have taken with an older uncle. One morning he hadn't got up and I just opened the door and took a shot at him with a sponge; he jumped out of bed, seized the watering-can that operated as a jug, and turned it upside-down over my head on the floor. It caused some consternation, as it went straight through the floor to the kitchen.

Playboy in more senses than one. He could play the fiddle, the flute, the penny whistle, the piano. Indeed he won a scholarship in harmony and counterpoint at the Royal Academy of Music. Partly it was his inheritance. For the story goes that an ancestor, John Millington, a canon or precentor of the Chapel Royal, sang so sweetly that Henry VIII bade him take the name of Sing. Stephen McKenna [sic][7] told George Roberts[8]

that Synge had little respect for the English, but he had great respect for the Synge family and loved to quote from his ancestor, the Archbishop. He hated the idea of the English in Ireland—except for the Synges. He thought the English a heavy and bovine people 'who had achieved a great literature by a mystery.'

Synge had in him that Irish split, that dichotomy, which produced so many fork-tongued writers—Congreve, Farquhar, Goldsmith, Sheridan, Shaw. He was Anglo-Irish; a Protestant in a Catholic country; a disbeliever reared in a devout envionment; a Puritan and a playboy; a University prizeman in Hebrew on the one hand and Gaelic on the other. Between the blades of these scissors he cut the cloth of drama, the many-coloured coat of comedy. Sharpness was all. But to arrive at this sharpness he had first, like many of his countrymen, to leave Ireland. At the age of twenty-one he went to Germany to study music.[9] *His mother, who looked askance at the stage and the platform, did not approve.*

STEPHENS: But she was always judicious. And when he decided that music ought to be his career she was quite willing to back him up. At the time he did that he hadn't got any money of his own at all.

Two years later Synge gave up his musical career and went to Paris on £40 a year.

STEPHENS: He had about that amount of money as private means and he used to make a few guineas more writing articles. His real home was his mother's house, and he used to stay in Paris, when he wanted to be there, as long as his money lasted, then he'd come home again. His mother was always trying to persuade him to come home because she said he didn't feed himself properly.

'I went to Paris,' said Synge to a friend, 'in order to be quiet, and to wear dirty clothes if I liked.' Stephen McKenna, who met him there, said that Synge told him he had laboured over one article for six weeks and was paid a guinea for it. Said McKenna, 'Oh, he complained about his lack of earning power, but he seemed more concerned at finding two sentences ending with the same cadence when his article was at last published. No, he hadn't a great knowledge of French. I was once about to buy a French encyclopaedia, and Synge said, "Don't buy it. Get the Encyclopaedia Britannica, *where the writer won't stop in the middle of an article to tell you how fond he is of his mother."' His family didn't much approve of his writing.*

STEPHENS: They thought it was an unprofitable enterprise. Their attitude was, 'Well, if he wants to write, why doesn't he write something that he can sell?'

Synge—so McKenna told George Roberts—had only one room in Paris, meagrely furnished with a truckle bed, a few chairs, a piece of old carpet and a few books and pipes. He did his typewriting with the typewriter on his knees. He had two small bowls for tea and if any more than two friends called to see him one of the company would have to wait till there was an empty bowl.

RICHARD BEST:[10] I remember one morning Stephens McKenna sent me

a card, and told me there was a friend of his called Synge going over to Paris. He was a very literary man, he had £40 a year—I remember the sum perfectly well, it seemed to me enormous at the time. Days passed and weeks passed, and I remember one morning awaking in my little flat, looking round my room, which was in perhaps a little disorder, and expressing to myself the hope that this man Synge wouldn't walk in now. I had hardly thought the thought when I heard a knock at my outer door. I thought it was the concierge coming with something, so I went to the door and there I saw a stranger standing before me with a white silk muffler round his neck, and he said to me in French, 'Vous êtes M. Best?' I said, 'Je le suis,' and he said, 'Je suis Synge—pas singe.' So I said, 'Come in, why should we speak French? I'm expecting you.'

We became quite friendly then, and I saw a good deal of Synge. After a time I induced him, as he had only £40 a year, not to be living in a furnished hotel but to set up in a little flat as I myself had. After six months or so I moved out of my flat, taking another one, and I installed him in my old flat, gave him a carpet and went out with him and bought all the necessary things—a bed, some blankets and all that; and I shall never forget I said to him, 'Must have a teapot, Synge.' So we saw some teapots—there was one blue and white; I said, 'Well, now, that would be a nice teapot,' and Synge said, 'Oh, no, I prefer that one—the little humble chocolate-coloured teapot.' So then I inducted him into the way of making tea and all that, and cooking a chop.

Synge, said McKenna, loved Paris. He loved the quiet of it and its tranquil bourgeoisie. He never belonged to the Latin Quarter or to the cabarets. Sometimes he would go to a café and just look on. His favourite walk was from his rooms to the Luxembourg—a long, tree-shaded walk called 'the Poets' Walk'. And he liked, too, the lovely villages on the outskirts of Paris and he loved their names. The boulevards he didn't know or care about. He hated big avenues and chose those which were narrow and winding.

BEST: I remember another curious meeting with Synge in Paris. We were walking down the Avenue de L'Opéra one sunny day and I saw a man coming towards us whom I recognised—a portly man, with a bowler hat and a plain suit. I had just time to say to Synge, 'Mark this man,' because he was on us almost. Synge looked at him, and I looked at him, and this man looked at us very closely, and I said, 'Oscar Wilde,' and Synge said, 'Oh, how interesting, let us go back and meet him again.' I hated this, but Wilde had stopped I remember, and was looking into a big window with Greek vases in it and bronzes. So we turned around and we met him again, a minute afterwards, and Wilde looked at us hard, and I knew Wilde was thinking, 'These two men know who I am.' He was living under the name Sebastian[11]—he had been pointed out to me some months before in the street, that's how I knew him. So I took him in, but I lowered my eyes and I noticed his brick-coloured complexion and his stained teeth which have

been described. Well, Synge was immensely impressed by this appearance of Wilde.

He had an immense curiosity about person, place or thing; little escaped him. He would spend hours in the Louvre and he would point out with unerring instinct some little detail of distinction in a picture which others mightn't notice.[12]

'Once,' said McKenna, 'I gave him some reproductions of Burne-Jones[13] and Watts,[14] about whose work I was then enthusiastic. I fancied that I saw in the painting of a hand, the fold of a drapery, an expression of a new sense of mysticism in the world. Synge got furiously angry, stammering and stuttering as he protested that a man who saw such a thing in that work knew nothing about pictures. He took me to the Louvre and going round the galleries he analysed the qualities of the pictures one by one. He wouldn't let me speak until I had soaked them in, and then he said, "Now where's your Burne-Jones and your Watts and all the rest of them?" He thought that no one's criticism of painting was worth listening to if they hadn't a technical knowledge of the subject, and the same with music.'

BEST: I myself was a dilettante—a dabbler in music. I remember I had Beethoven's piano sonatas, and one day Synge opened it at one of the sonatas and pointed out to me the theme and how it developed and varied through the different movements. He played the violin and he had a way of drumming on the table to strengthen his fingers for the violin.

A habit which annoyed his mother. Synge had a wide and wandering interest in the arts, in music, painting, sculpture, writing, coins and medallions, prints and engravings. But it was a choosy, intuitive interest, not an intellectual interest: a 'negative capability'. 'Sometimes,' said McKenna, 'I would read Yeats's poems to Synge in Paris. I read "The Shadowy Waters" with Synge. He thought it obscure but beautiful; one of the most beautiful things that had ever been written. And yet when he was offered the book he refused it. "I might understand it," he said. He preferred diffuseness to definition.'

Because it gave room and rein to imagination. He would have agreed with Coleridge that 'poetry gives most pleasure when only generally and not perfectly understood'. He disliked being pinned down by intellect. He liked to wander, whether in the body or in spirit, in life or in letters. But this wide scattering at last found a narrow gathering. In 1898, on the advice of a friend,[15] *Synge packed his bags. 'Give up Paris,' he was told. 'You will never create anything by reading Racine, and Arthur Symons will always be a better critic of French literature. Go to the Aran Islands. Live there as if you were one of the people themselves. Express a life that has never found expression.' He took the advice. And yet, says Seamus O'Sullivan—*

O'SULLIVAN: Synge had, to the end of his life, a real love of Paris, that Paris to which he had first gone (as he confided to me one evening as we walked home from the Camden Hall to his lodgings in Rathmines) in order to free himself from the influence—an influence which he felt was becoming too strong—of the Irish poet who at that time, and for many years afterwards, dominated the thought and expression of the younger

writers of his day. 'Get away from Dublin,' he said to me as we parted after a memorable walk and talk.

Strange. For it was that same dominating Irish poet, Yeats, who advised Synge to 'get away from Paris', to go to Aran. It was on Aran that Synge found a frame for his hiving imagination. It was in that bare, primitive, hand-to-mouth place that he, who had such riches of imagination, such endless means and meaningless ends, found peace and purpose.

BEST: I remember Synge telling me that he wanted to do for the Aran Islands something like what Pierre Loti had done for Brittany. I thought it was rather a tall order, and I smiled. But he didn't write then the ordinary English with any distinction. It was when he discovered his Aran Island dialect that Synge found himself.

'Yeats,' said George Moore, 'trained him through dialect: he dunged the roots.' Years earlier, Stephen Crane[16] had roused Synge's interest in islands. And Synge, as Edward Stephens points out, had also a family association with Aran.

STEPHENS: John's uncle, his father's brother, Alec Synge, was the Protestant curate there about 1850. He had a sailing-boat for carrying on his ministrations between the islands and he used it for fishing when he wasn't on religious work and so he got into a pretty serious conflict with the fishermen of Galway. But he wasn't a man to give in; he armed the skipper to the teeth, and so long as he was there he fished.

Dignity, with impudence in the pocket; peace, with violence at its heart. It was this sharp counterpoint of life on Aran that gave Synge, that sober, melancholy man, a heightened sense of drama, and a supreme sense of comedy. He revisited the islands, and particularly the middle island, in five successive autumns. And always, whether sitting on the cliff above or in the kitchen below, he was the shy observer, the silent listener, the stranger. One night, about two years ago, on the middle island I listened to Peadar Coneely telling a story in Gaelic, and this is a translation of it:
'When O'Malley came on the run here long ago he had killed his father by accident. He was working in the field, and his father came and checked him—said that he was spoiling the field. Dispute arose between them, and in anger he lifted the spade over his head; he didn't intend to kill him, but with anger he gave the blow contrarily, and killed the father. After doing it he was attending the father—it hurt himself more than most others—but he didn't intend to leave the place, only an uncle of his told him to go on the run and save himself. The uncle sent a boat into Aran with him . . .'
It is the story that John Synge heard from old Pandeen Derrane, and out of which he fashioned The Playboy of the Western World.

Richard Best talked once to Synge about his life on Aran.

BEST: He told me how embarrassed he used to be when he went there first. Synge had a little room off the kitchen, where he used to sleep. In the daytime, when he had to obey a call of nature—there were no up-to-date

lavatories—he told me rather shyly that he used to go out into a field, overlooking the wild Atlantic, and just when he would be about to perform the major operation he would look round to see if there was anybody nearby; and nearly always, he said, some young woman would put her head over the stone wall. So I said, 'What did you do?' 'Well,' he said, 'I used to postpone that part of my daily routine until night. Then when the inmates of the house were all asleep, I would open my door and steal out over their bunks into the darkness of night.' I often wondered if that wasn't in some way responsible for the illness which eventually carried him off.

'Did you ever think,' said an Aran Islander to me, 'that there was something simple about Synge? There was a wonderment about him that was very fetching.' Synge was not one of those nimble Irishmen who could turn a bicycle on a sixpence or turn a phrase like a corkscrew. He loathed the 'brilliant' talker, and, as Gogarty says, he was a drinker-in and not a giver-out of talk.

OLIVER ST JOHN GOGARTY:[17] The greatest thing I can think about Synge is how he affected the present Poet Laureate, John Masefield.[18] They were fast friends, and the man must have been pretty worthy and Masefield must have been of an affectionate and winning type, or he would not have gained the friendship of that, to me, inscrutable man. In order to summon Synge to your mind's eye, I'd better read a quotation from John Masefield's *Recent Prose*. 'It was a grave dark face, with a good deal in it, the hair was worn neither long nor short; the moustache was rather thick and heavy, the lower jaw, otherwise clean shaven, was made remarkable by a tuft of hair too small to be called a goatee on the lower lip. The head was a good size. There was nothing niggardly, nothing abundant about it. The face was pale, the cheeks were rather drawn; in my memory they were rather seamed and old-looking. The eyes were at once smoky and kindling. The mouth, not well seen below the moustache, had a great play of humour in it.'

He had a face like a blacking-brush, said Bernard Shaw.

GOGARTY: But for this humorous mouth, the kindling in the eyes, and something not robust in his build, he would have been more like a Scotsman than an Irishman. I remember wondering if he were Irish. His voice, very guttural and quick with a kind of lively bitterness in it, was of a kind of Irish voice new to me at the time. I've known a good many Irish people but they'd all been vivacious and picturesque, rapid in intellectual argument, and vague about life. There was nothing vivacious, picturesque, rapid or vague about Synge. The rush-bottomed chair next to him was filled by talker after talker, but Synge was not talking. He was answering.

He was always the hole in the conversation. 'Sometimes I thought there was nothing in him,' said a friend, and he spoke of himself as 'existing merely in his perception of the

waves and of the crying birds and the smell of seaweed.' He was a silent traveller, as his nephew Edward Stephens says.

STEPHENS: He was never in the least embarrassed by walking in silence. None of his family were. It wasn't a peculiarity of him particularly, the Synges were like that, they were a silent family.

Silent but expressive. 'They speak, but not with their mouths,' says the Psalmist. Synge's hands, for example, spoke for him.

STEPHENS: He'd a peculiar dexterity that was particularly noticeable in the hands of a man as thick-set and powerful as he was. It was a natural gift, perhaps a mode of expression is a better description. As a boy he had made a collection of butterflies, moths and beetles. He had a setting-house full of cork-covered, grooved boards of all sizes, for setting the wings and antennae and legs of specimens. And that required a considerable dexterity. He made a very neat collection. Then his fingers acquired even greater dexterity when he learnt the violin and the piano. He had a personal habit, too, of whirling a small pair of pocket scissors on his finger as he'd saunter about the house chanting 'Holy, Holy, Holy Moses'. I think he always said 'Holy Moses' because his mother wouldn't have liked him to use any stronger terms.

The way his hands moved impressed me very much as a child when I saw him putting his violin carefully into its case, spreading a silk handkerchief gently over it, putting the bow into position, and putting down the lid and fastening the catches. He used to pride himself on his tricks of dexterity. For instance, he used to stand on one foot, put a bunch of keys next to his instep and then, with his arm twisted round his leg, pick up the keys. He was very good at handling fishing tackle, and he used to tie flies when he was a boy. I used to fish with him in the evenings along the river until we couldn't see our tackle, except by holding it against the sky. He could always put on a new fly if one was lost or untangle a cast. He didn't carry much tackle—the cast round his hat and an old wallet with some bluebottle, a hare's ear, an orange spider and a few other flies regularly used on Wicklow rivers. He never wore waders—he used usually to put on a pair of old shoes, and walk in the water just the same as if it was dry land. I have a picture in my mind of him standing nearly ankle-deep in the river, bending slightly, and casting down a dark hole under bushes. I remember the squelch of our feet walking home, and the bats circling round the tops of our heads.

BEST: I remember in those far-off days that Synge wore rather coarse, hand-knitted socks, and he told me that his mother knitted them for him.

'And I remember,' says George Roberts, 'going on an outing with Synge to Lough Bray.'

GEORGE ROBERTS: We rested by a stream in a little wood about half-way

up the glen and one of the party, Maire ni Garvey, leaned back amongst some flowers, which Synge described as 'stretched back until her necklace, in the flowers of the earth', and later on he used the phrase in *The Playboy*. This was an instance of how he noted every event on every occasion. We were lucky that the day was full of change and as we looked at the sunlit lake it reflected the blue of the sky in all its peace and repose. But a change in the atmosphere provoked a gloomy background and I mentioned to Synge that I sensed an evil emanation, to which he agreed. He said he had experienced a sense of the evil when swimming across the lake.

The Shadow of the Glen. Gaiety and gloom, light and dark, freedom and frustration, the play of counterpoint in all Synge's life and works. Was it this incident that Synge had in mind when he called his first play The Shadow of the Glen? *Yeats was deeply impressed with the play and mentioned it to Richard Best.*

BEST: I was sitting on a bench beside him and Yeats said to me in that impressive way—intoning his words—that he had just discovered a man who had all the talent of Aeschylus and Sophocles combined. I said to him, 'How wonderful, who is he?' 'He is a man of the name of Synge.' 'Hang it all,' I said. 'I just tore up his letters the other day—I wish I had known before that.' And Yeats laughed. Well, that was Synge—I think he had just written *The Wicklow Glen,* but it was Yeats who really discovered a latent talent in Synge, and encouraged him to go on writing.

George Roberts was present when Yeats brought Synge to meet the members of the National Theatre Society.

ROBERTS: He was present at his election and I remember well his genuine look of pleasure as he courteously thanked us. He attended many of the rehearsals of *The Shadow of the Glen,* giving us the rhythm of the speech, but he left the stage management entirely in the hands of W. G. Fay. Although this was his first play he altered practically nothing at rehearsals and was not in the slightest bit fussy or irritable.

 The Shadow of the Glen was first performed in the Molesworth Hall on 8 October 1903 and it got a rather mixed reception.[19] There were calls for the author, but when he appeared there were a few hisses. His nervousness at facing an audience even to bow was plain to everybody, but when he heard the hisses a glimpse of defiant pleasure came over his face. I think the hisses pleased him much more than the applause.

The play started a heated newspaper controversy. But Synge took no part in it. He was always averse to defending his work, even to his friends. 'I follow Goethe's rule,' he said, 'to tell no one what one means in one's writing.'

ROBERTS: Although Synge never asserted his belief in his own powers he was quite conscious of his gifts. I remember his being hugely amused by a friend who had heard of the performance of his first play and who sent him a whole library of German plays so that he 'might learn how to write a

play'. This reserve passed with many for modesty, but like all great artists he was very far from being self-deprecatory. His lack of self-assertion came rather from quiet confidence that his work was good.

'Good artists,' said Oscar Wilde, 'don't care for each other's work!' 'I never knew,' said Yeats, 'if Synge cared for work of mine, and do not remember that I had from him even a conventional compliment.'

GOGARTY: He was extremely self-possessed, not at all an amiable person, not an offensive person, nor deliberately self-obliterating.

ROBERTS: The next of Synge's plays produced was *Riders to the Sea*, and Synge was very particular that every detail of the properties and costumes should be correct. The petticoats were made under his direction with a broad strip of calico at the top. The pampooties were another difficulty. Synge brought in a pair used in the Aran Islands to show how they were made. The spinning-wheel was another trouble, until Lady Gregory came to the rescue and sent up a large wheel from Galway. Synge himself instructed the girl how to use it. He was exceedingly anxious that the 'caoine'[20] should be as close as possible to the peculiar chant that is used in the Islands and after much searching I found a Galway woman living in one of the Dublin suburbs who consented to show one of the girls how the caoine was given.

She was very nervous about it, though somewhat proud that what she looked on as a country custom should be so eagerly sought after in the city. At the same time, she was very interested in the whole affair, wanting to know what the play was about and saying the caoine was so terrible a thing that she could hardly believe people would want to put it in a play. At first she tried to begin in her little parlour, but she confessed after a few moments she could not do it properly there, so she brought the two girls up to a bedroom and at first it seemed no better, until she conceived the idea that I should act the corpse. She lighted the candles for the wake and then she got that note full of the terror of the dead. I was relieved that she did not take snuff off my belly, but apparently the candles were enough. She was a native Irish speaker and the Irish cadences and rhythm of the words in conjunction with the clapping of her hands and swaying of her body was very terrible and yet very beautiful to look on.

It was George Moore who congratulated Synge on having made great literature out of a barbaric peasant jargon. But many Irishmen, like Gogarty, accuse Synge of inventing a fake peasant language.

GOGARTY: This language I have never heard in the mouth of any countryman in Ireland. It is an ersatz, which has been credited with much simplcity and beauty, but which always offended me by its artificiality.

'Yet,' protested Synge, 'I have used one or two words only that I have not heard among the country people of Ireland.' His nephew explains—

STEPHENS: He used to work in his bedroom, and his bedroom was in a little return where there was only a boarded floor on joists. There was no ceiling and he hammered away upstairs and the door was lying open into the yard. Fellows working on the farm used to pass the door, and the girls used to chat with them as they passed. He naturally heard the conversation upstairs, and he says that he owes lots of that for the phrases he used in the *Shadow of the Glen*.

When he was writing the *Shadow of the Glen* I remember we walked up the old Carrow road. It had stopped raining, but the fog was down on the hills, and it was one of those days when everything appears enlarged by a fog. Bushes up on the ditch looked as if they were trees, and every sheep that jumped across the road looked fabulously large. Of course my brother began to exaggerate and say how extraordinarily large everything was, and Synge jeered at us as he always did, and when we saw a cottage he said, 'Now wouldn't you think that was a cathedral?' So when he got home he put all that into the mouth of the tramp—the tower and church and the city of Dublin is only another version of his joke on us.

He worked with his whole life as his material—and he always thought that an author shouldn't be a phrase-coiner. He loved living phrase. He liked to live among people who used living phrases, and he felt entitled, in fact bound, to make use of the phrases just as he heard them.

ROBERTS: Before he ever started writing a play he had filled many notebooks with phrases he had heard; many of them collected quite near Dublin on cycle rides in County Wicklow. He told me his usual practice was, when he saw anyone coming along with whom he wished to chat, to get off his bicycle and feign that something had gone wrong with it; the curiosity of the passer-by was almost invariably aroused and a conversation would inevitably follow.

Synge has been sometimes accused by his detractors of never having heard many of the speeches they objected to, but anyone who has come into contact with the country people and spoken to them on terms of comradeship knows how their imagination flares into great extravagance of speech. For instance a friend of mine overheard a woman whose child had stolen a piece of sugar cry out at him, 'May the hammers of damnation beat out the soul of you on the anvil of hell.' I told that to Synge and he was delighted.

Was Synge a hard worker, Mr Stephens?

STEPHENS: He wasn't a worker who worked at night. He generally worked in the morning between breakfast and lunch. But you couldn't say for certain. He disposed of his day as he felt. He used to say that a man worked according to his humour; he believed in the effect of moods, and he would fit in his work while he felt like doing it. Once he'd got a thing in his mind he would stick at it till he had it right, and nothing but perfection

would satisfy him. He would get a thing as perfect as he could make it. In fact, some people said he had too high a standard, that he delayed himself by his extreme care, even minding about a pause. He used to come up and sit in our garden sometimes, when he was writing *The Playboy*. And I remember him saying a man can't work with the cream of his brain for more than six hours a day.

ROBERTS: He was always a very slow writer, owing to the number of versions he made before he would be satisfied. His method was to work direct on to the typewriter from his first rough notes. He would take his typescript and make alterations in ink until it became covered, then make a fresh copy. Version after version of each play was thus made before it reached its final form. He seldom made alterations once the play was put into rehearsal and this, of course, was of great benefit to the actors. No doubt his constant attendance at rehearsals helped him to avoid the mistakes which other dramatists might be prone to.

It was at rehearsal that Gogarty met Synge.

GOGARTY: The first time I came across him was in a little hall, off Camden Street in Dublin, where a rehearsal of his *Playboy* was about to take place.

James Joyce couldn't be kept away from the theatre any more than moths from a flame. He insisted on coming to the rehearsal, although we were neither of us invited, but he was overcome in the corridor, and he lay down, so I passed on and I said to Synge, 'This play you've written is a satire, surely.' The playboy becomes very famous because he's presumed to have killed his father. Later his father turns up, and the playboy is discredited. I said, 'Surely this is a satire on the want of action in Irish life.' He looked at me very grimly and broke silence, which he rarely did, and said, 'No. It's a work of art.' So he resumed his position, which consisted of sitting down with his two hands folded on the top of a walking-stick, and his chin resting on it.

The reason I wasn't well received was probably that he associated me with Joyce, who was at that moment lying in the fairway and obstructing any of the people who came to see the rehearsal. Joyce afterwards confessed that he didn't mind at all the position, provided the girls stepped over his form. Then Joyce was presumed to have insulted the doorway of Synge's mother's house at Glenageary so that we cannot be said to have been very close friends of Synge.

Seamus O'Sullivan, also, met Synge at rehearsals.

O'SULLIVAN: Others were there who were then making a name in literature, art or music, but even in that distinguished company, Synge was a figure which caught and held the attention. For, apart from the strong and deeply lined features—the features of a man who had suffered much—there was in his appearance something which set him apart from

all the rest. He still wore the black cape-coat of his Parisian days, and this combined with the unmistakable perfume of the Caporal tobacco which he smoked continuously in cigarettes which he rolled in the French fashion, without the aid of any machine, gave, to some of us at least, a nostalgic memory of Paris and of the Latin Quarter.

He always, says Dossy Wright,[21] *kept to himself at rehearsals.*

DOSSY WRIGHT: I always found him very reserved, even in meeting people when a rehearsal was over, or when we had a talking round after rehearsal, when most of the people stayed behind in the Camden Street Hall, Synge didn't stay very long. He always seemed to be in a hurry to get back to his home.

The Company moved to the new theatre, the Abbey, in 1904, and Synge was made a director.[22] *Fred O'Donovan*[23] *recalls his first meeting there with Synge and remarks on the reticence.*

FRED O'DONOVAN: Yes, that was very typical of the man. We had one of our little parties after a matinée, and we came into the Green Room. Synge was there, Lady Gregory and Yeats. Lady Gregory was in one corner of the room, surrounded by her admirers, and Yeats was standing in the centre of the room holding forth very magnificently, surrounded by his worshippers, and then there was this quiet figure, sitting behind the hat-rack in the corner, and I remember distinctly seeing beads of perspiration on his forehead. Nobody taking any notice of him, everybody around Yeats and Lady Gregory—and the man behind the hat-rack was Synge, and I could see on his face he had one great desire, and that was to escape from the room as quickly and unobtrusively as possible.

WRIGHT: He became rather interested in Mollie O'Neill,[24] and then he used to go off afterwards, and Mollie went off with him. I don't think in those days the other directors realised where he was going, or who was meeting him. But Lady Gregory got her suspicions some way or another and found out, and then she was a bit perturbed for a while because at one time she said to me, 'You know, Dossy, it would be very awkward if one of the actresses here became a wife of one of our directors.'

O'DONOVAN: She was very beautiful, in an Irish fashion, very attractive in her personality, and a brilliant actress. Wherever we went she seemed to capture everybody, and I know she was, in Synge's opinion and in the opinion of our audiences, the embodiment of Pegeen Mike in *The Playboy*.

In 1907, as George Roberts recalls it, came the famous first production of The Playboy of the Western World.

ROBERTS: Synge mentioned to W. G. Fay one day in the Green Room that he had started to write a new play about the man who killed his father. 'You will have to play the murderer,' he said to Fay with that peculiar

sibilant laugh of his. Well, Synge arranged to publish *The Playboy of the Western World* with me, and in good time I got the MS. It was complete in final form. He brought the MS himself to Maunsel's office and after a hasty reading I expressed my wild enthusiasm for the work to him. I remember the look of pleasure that my excited emotion gave him. His countenance 'put on the light of children praised'. He was excessively sensitive to any appreciation which he knew to be sincere, but just as scornful and quick to detect mere politeness.

The play went into rehearsal at once and the first to demur at some of the speeches were some of the cast. He told me that one speech would have to be cut for the performance and a speech modified, and he said with a twinkle in his eye, 'but *you* must print it as it is *written*,' well knowing that I did not want to cut a word of it.

The next protest came from the printer who begged me to leave out the word 'bloody' (this was before Shaw's memorable use of it). The printer was much shocked at what he called the 'blasphemous' passages. He was on the verge of refusing to print it but was at last persuaded.

Synge himself directed the rehearsals, regardless of J. B. Yeats who was busy sketching him.

ROBERTS: Yet the result was one of Yeats's best efforts and it is undoubtedly the real Synge more than any other portrait. His hat was pushed back from his forehead, from which the sweat was literally pouring, as it always did under any excitement. He was excited under nervous strain at the final rehearsals of his work. When the sketch was being made, Molly O'Neill, who was not on the stage, and was a very interested spectator of the artist's progress, would alternately look over the artist's shoulder at the sketch and at the subject of the sketch. The look she gave Synge as he turned for a moment from watching the rehearsal to look at the sketch amply repaid him for the interruption.

There was not a vacant seat on the night of the first performance of The Playboy.

ROBERTS: The first act was listened to with tense silence and vigorously applauded, although it contained some of the phrases which Synge's enemies subsequently denounced. During the second act there was an uneasy atmosphere in the house and at the end there was a scrappy applause, but there was no outcry until near the end of the act, when Christy Mahon speaks of 'a drift of mountain females standing in their shifts only', at which someone in the pit hissed. A lot of the audience joined in expressing disapproval and a few tried to quell the disturbance. There was a slight lull. Then it broke out again with redoubled fury and feet were stamped and at the same time there was unusually vociferous applause. Between the two groups not a word could be heard, though the players went on till the curtain fell. There were some calls for 'author' but Synge, who was in the back row of the stalls, kept his seat. He was talking to AE as

the house emptied, looking defiant and also somewhat concerned at the hostile reception.

The next morning the papers were filled with the vilest abuse I have ever read, masquerading as criticism. The *Freeman's Journal* was rather comic when it sympathised with Miss Allgood at having to say a word that it was sure she would blush to utter even in the privacy of her bedroom. The word was 'shift'.

The next night there were very few people in the stalls, but the pit was full of young men, Gaelic Leaguers[25] and members of Nationalist clubs who, to judge by their faces and scraps of angry conversations overheard before the curtain rose, had come with one intention, to stop the performance. The first act had hardly begun when hisses and booing started. The actors continued to play, but the crowd got more angry and started a continuous stamping of feet to the rhythm of what is known as Kentish fire, so that no words could possibly be heard. But the actors went bravely on. Though their lips could be seen moving, no sound reached the audience. Synge was very much concerned, for fear the audience would begin to throw things at the players, and he insisted on going into the pit, I believe with the intention of preventing anyone who attempted more active violence. I went with him, and presently he was recognised. Damns and curses were heaped on him in language just as strong, and in some instances nearly as picturesque as the words of the play they objected to. In the middle of the commotion I noticed a gleam of humour come into his eye, as he took a mental note of a specially violent curse.

The fact that the players kept on with the script seemed to have an extraordinary effect on the audience and their frustrated fury was getting dangerous, especially as they now fixed their attention on Synge and seemed to ignore the players. They turned round from their seats in the front, yelling, and shook their fists in Synge's face. He sat for a while quite calmly, but with a fixed look of hatred gathering on his face and his jaw set. I began to be afraid he was going to try to clear the pit himself and of course any physical opposition on his part would only give some of his enemies the excuse they longed for. I tried to persuade him to leave but he insisted on staying till the close of the act. We then went to the Green Room of the theatre to encourage the players. As the curtain was about to go up for the third act, Synge was again making his way to the pit. The charwoman of the theatre came to him crying, 'For the love of God, don't go near the pit again. They will kill you.' This amused him so much that he could not resist her appeal and he stayed behind the scenes.

Just as the play was over Yeats arrived. He burst into the Green Room where the company were assembled, with the gleam of battle in his eye. 'This is the best thing that ever happened in my life,' said he. His only fear was that the players would refuse to go on the remaining nights of the week that the play was booked for.

'Synge,' said Yeats, 'came and stood beside me and said, "A young doctor has just told me that he can hardly keep himself from jumping onto a seat, and pointing out in that howling mob those whom he is treating for venereal disease."'

ROBERTS: The rest of the performances turned themselves into a duel between the actors and the audience. The actors made a point of shouting out the speeches the audiences most objected to, and sometimes they made themselves heard above the din.

Poor Synge was laid up after this night and did not come to the theatre till after the week was over. It is hard to say what the real effect was on him. He professed indifference, tinged with amusement. But when the garbled reports appeared in the country papers he said to me he was concerned that some of these might penetrate to the Aran Islands and that this misrepresentation might prejudice the people on whom he looked with affection. He said, 'Perhaps they will not receive me so kindly when I go there again.' I think it was this dread that stopped him from visiting his beloved islands again.

'The Playboy's real name was Synge,' said Bernard Shaw, 'and the famous libel on Ireland (and who is Ireland that she should not be libelled as other countries by her great comedians?) was the truth about the world.' It was Synge's last home-truth, and its reception told sorely on him. Disappointment and sickness turned him in on himself, and his work began to take on a more personal, tragic and poetic tinge in Deirdre of the Sorrows. *One evening George Roberts went to hear him read some poems in his mother's house at Kingstown.*

ROBERTS: He seemed unusually perturbed even before starting to read, and when he began, his voice was so full of nervousness that it was difficult to follow the poems. As he read, however, he became more violently excited than I had ever seen him. He seemed to get back the original motive and mood of the poems he was reading. It was hard to keep one's critical faculties alive under those circumstances. He seemed to be very weary and exhausted with reading them, but he said, 'I will send them to Yeats; I won't read them to him—it's too much expense of spirit.' It was very late when we had finished and as Synge got up to let me out he asked me to go noiselessly lest I should disturb his mother.

In October 1908, Synge's mother died. 'I remember,' says Richard Best, 'the house at Kingstown.'

BEST: I remember the last time I was there with him he took me into the kitchen where he was preparing on the range—his mother was dead—some sour milk tablets, prescribed by Metchnikoff, the great Russian bacteriologist, as a cure for old age. We arranged that I was to go down the next fortnight, and I was told he was in Elpis, the nursing home, so I saw him there. He had grown a beard in the meantime and I remember Synge telling me of his plans, how in a month or so, when he

would be out of Elpis, what he was going to do. But he didn't tell me that he was going to be married. And I thought he was searching my countenance, but I felt then that he never would leave . . . that he was a dying man. I said nothing.

One of the hospital staff spoke about Synge to George Roberts, who noted the conversation at the time.

ROBERTS: Just before he died he kept murmuring in his delirium, 'God have mercy on me. God forgive me.' His favourite nurse was a Catholic and used to make him say his prayers each night and morning. She used to pray for him and he thanked God he had someone to pray for such a sinner. He called her his 'tidy nurse' because she was always immaculate when attending him. He liked her and she liked him, and did everything she could to make his last hours happy. Before he lost consciousness she sprinkled holy water over him and he opened his eyes to ask, 'Are you baptising me?' and added, 'perhaps it is best so.' Not being sure of heaven he used to say he'd like to remain as long as he could on earth.

He read portions of the Bible each day, but refused to see a minister or priest. When the matron did bring in a minister a few days before his death Synge chatted to him about the weather and other such-like topics. His 'tidy' nurse was of the opinion that he had much more religion than many who had more pretension to it. His relations called to inquire every day, but never went up to see him. He used to ask, 'Were any of my affectionate relatives here today?'

Edward Stephens, his nephew, went to see him.

STEPHENS: I saw him in Elpis Private Hospital the day before he died. I brought him a bottle of champagne sent by his brother Robert and a tap corkscrew for drawing out a small quantity. John had been moved two days before from a room overlooking Mount Street, to a sunny room at the back of the house, where there was a view of the mountains. When I saw him I was shocked by the change in his appearance, but as I was a student of twenty I had very little experience of serious illness, and I did not fully understand how near he was to death. He was too weak to talk at first, but the nurse screwed the tap into the cork of the bottle I'd brought, and gave him some champagne, and then he seemed a little brighter. He asked me whether I had heard any blackbirds singing. And I said, 'Not yet—but I have heard some thrushes.'

And Seamus O'Sullivan also had a kindly thought for John Synge.

O'SULLIVAN: I was told that he had expressed a wish to read again the poems of Robert Herrick, and I sent him by a friend that exquisite little selection which Palgrave published in the Golden Treasury series under the title of 'Chrysomela', and I like to fancy that the little volume was with him in those last days when, as we are told, he had had his bed moved to a

position from which he could see, however dimly, the Wicklow Hills. For there may have been a great deal in common between the gay Vicar of Deane Bourne who sang of

> Brooks, of Blossoms, Birds and Bowers:
> Of April, May, of June and July-flowers;
> ... Of May-poles, Hock-carts, Wassails, Wakes,
> Of Bride-grooms, Brides, and of their Bridal-Cakes

and the poet who walked with no unseeing eye through the hills and glens of Wicklow or lay dreaming on heathery places in Connemara 'and the ways beyond'.

'It is a pity,' said Synge, *'that I should die, for I still have more than one playboy in my belly.'*

NOTES

William Robert Rodgers (1909–69) was born in Belfast; became Presbyterian minister in Armagh (1934–46); BBC producer and scriptwriter (1946–52); and was elected to the Irish Academy of Letters as a distinguished Irish and Ulster poet (1951). His books include *Awake* (1941), *Europa and the Bull* (1952) and *Ireland in Colour* (1956). See Darcy O'Brien, *W. R. Rodgers (1909–1969)*, Irish Writers Series (Lewisburg: Bucknell University Press, 1970).

1. J. M. Synge, 'On an Anniversary', *Collected Works*, vol. I: *Poems*, ed. Robin Skelton (London: Oxford University Press, 1962) p. 33.
2. Seamus O'Sullivan (1879–1958), pen-name of James Sullivan Starkey, Irish poet; founder of *The Dublin Magazine* (1923); played a prominent part in the Irish literary revival; a friend of W. B. Yeats, AE, Oliver St John Gogarty, James Joyce and Arthur Griffith; and member of the Irish Academy of Letters.
3. Edward Millington Stephens, co-author of *J. M. Synge 1871–1909* (New York: Macmillan, 1959).
4. Synge's interest in nature persisted into his late adolescence. He joined the Dublin Naturalists' Field Club (founded 1886) and remained a member until 1888, though he wrote no papers for it.
5. In some autobiographical notes Synge made in Paris, he described a spiritual crisis caused by reading Charles Darwin. See *Collected Works*, vol. II: *Prose*, ed. Alan Price (London and New York: Oxford University Press, 1966) p. 10, and Edward Stephens, *My Uncle John*, op. cit., pp. 36–7.
6. Cherrie Matheson [Mrs C. H. Houghton]. See her previous memoir, 'John Synge as I Knew Him', p. 3.
7. Synge's Paris literary friend. See his previous memoir, 'Synge', p. 14.
8. The managing editor of Maunsel and Co., which published *The Works of John M. Synge*. He also created the part of Timmy in Synge's *The Well of the Saints*. See his article, 'A National Dramatist', *Shanachie* (Dublin) (Mar 1907) p. 57. Among the manuscript holdings in the National Library of Ireland are 'The Roberts Papers'.
9. It was Mary Synge, an English cousin of Synge's father and a concert pianist, who during a visit to Dublin in March 1893 persuaded the family that Synge should go to Germany to continue his musical studies. At the end of July 1893 he left Ireland for London, where he met Mary Synge, and together they travelled to Coblenz.
10. For a note on Dr Richard Best see p. 47.
11. At the peak of Oscar Wilde's success came disaster. He had become intimate with Lord

Alfred Douglas, son of the Marquis of Queensberry. The Marquis publicly accused Wilde of homosexual practices, and Wilde rashly brought suit for libel. He lost the suit, was arrested and convicted on the morals charge, and served two years in Reading Gaol (1895–7). A broken man, he spent his last years on the Continent.

12. Synge was always very fond of pictures; he actually attempted painting, and for many years was a member of the United Arts Club, Dublin.

13. Sir Edward Coley Burne-Jones (1833–98), one of the leading painters and designers of late nineteenth-century England, whose romantic, pseudo-medieval paintings were among the last manifestations of the Pre-Raphaelite style.

14. George Frederic Watts (1817–1904), English painter and sculptor of grandiose allegorical themes.

15. W. B. Yeats.

16. Stephen Crane (1871–1900), American novelist, poet and short-story writer regarded as a pioneer of Naturalism in American literature. His works include *The Red Badge of Courage* (1895) and *The Open Boat and Other Tales of Adventure* (1898).

17. For a note on Oliver St John Gogarty see p. 35.

18. For a note on John Masefield see p. 85.

19. Synge's first play, *In the Shadow of the Glen*, begins the series of grave, original studies of Irish character and thought which from time to time drew upon Synge the hostility of his audiences, but are now appreciated wherever Irish drama is played.

20. Keen.

21. 'Adolphus Wright has been with the Theatre for . . . many years. . . . He acted very often in the earliest productions, he knows our Theatre through and through, since he first appeared as a mere helper in Camden Street, then he followed the little Company to Molesworth Hall, then to the Abbey Theatre, and today, February 1950, I have seen . . . Dossie Wright directing how our new piano should be placed.'—Lennox Robinson, *Ireland's Abbey Theatre* (London: Sidgwick and Jackson, 1951) p. 66.

22. Synge became a Director of the Irish National Theatre Society in 1905, not in 1904.

23. Well-known actor in the early days of the Abbey Theatre. He took the part of Christy Mahon in the first production of *The Playboy of the Western World* in America and of Naisi in the first production of *Deirdre of the Sorrows* at the Abbey Theatre.

24. Molly Allgood ['Maire O'Neill']. For a note on her see p. 73.

25. For a note on the Gaelic League see p. 15. Synge loathed the idea of 'movements' or 'schools'. He wanted individual writers, and said that one of his young Irish fellow dramatists had lost a good deal of his talent by joining the Gaelic League.

Memories of John Synge*

WALTER STARKIE

A declining septuagenarian is left with little else to do but rummage fitfully through the dusty lumber-room of memory. Whether this is a sign of approaching second childhood or not, I find the incidents which come easily and clearly to my mind and the personalities who press upon me most closely are those of three score years ago. Hence my resolve to set down some of my memories of John Millington Synge and of Jack B. Yeats, whose centenaries we are celebrating this year.

Synge when I knew him (I was ten years of age) lived in Crosthwaite Park, Kingstown (now Dun Laoghaire), next door to the house where my grandmother lived. I used to watch him strolling along the Dalkey road, swinging his stick, and would wonder whether he was French or Austrian, for he had a moustache and a little goatee or 'imperial'. He was a lonely man wrapped in his thoughts and I hardly dared to open my lips when he greeted me. He became for me a man of mystery when one night I heard him playing his fiddle next door. In those days the fiddle had begun to fascinate me, for we had an Irish-speaking gardener at home in Killiney, called Drennan, who used to play Irish tunes for me by the hour and tell me tales of Finn,[1] Cuchulain[2] and Queen Maeve.[3]

Little did I know then that the lonely fiddler would give me the most exciting experience of my youth when in January 1907 his *Playboy of the Western World* was produced for the first time at the Abbey Theatre. My recollections of the acting on that occasion are hazy, for the real drama took place in the auditorium. From my seat at the side of the gallery I had a wonderful view of the milling mob. Suddenly the doors of the auditorium opened: a posse of Dublin Metropolitan Police entered and many of the rowdy elements were cast out. I have a vivid vision of Synge in the interval as he moved among the actors in the green room like a lost soul. His face was pale and sunken and he looked like the ghost of the sun-tanned wanderer I used to meet walking by the sea. It was my last sight of him, for two years later, when I was at school in Shrewsbury, my mother wrote telling me of his death.

Then during the Christmas holidays that year my friend Jack Larchet[4]

---

* *Yeats Studies; An International Journal*, no. 2 (1972) 91–5. Most of the material in this memoir was included in *Scholars and Gypsies; An Autobiography* (London: John Murray, 1963) pp. 82–5.

told me that they intended to produce for the first time, on 13 January 1910, Synge's unfinished tragedy, *Deirdre of the Sorrows*. When I look back over my memories I can remember no play that produced so deep an impression upon me as *Deirdre of the Sorrows*. I see clearly in my mind's eye the wild young princess gathering up her rich robes and jewels, and I hear her voice saying prophetically: 'I will dress like Emer[5] in Dundealgan, or Maeve in her house in Connaught. If Conchubor'll[6] make me a queen, I'll have the right of a queen who is master.' To me who had been accustomed to plod through a Greek tragedy word by word in class, *Deirdre of the Sorrows* was a revelation: it seemed as if some new kind of drama combining the qualities of the *Agamemnon* of Aeschylus and of *Antony and Cleopatra* had been conjured up before me by the ghost of the departed dramatist whom I had seen three years before in the rioting theatre, a forlorn figure in the midst of pandemonium. Later I was to learn from Yeats and Lady Gregory of Synge's race against death to finish the play and of his love for Molly Allgood, the young actress who played Deirdre. He was haunted by fears about his forthcoming marriage to Molly: he felt he was too old for her. Thus he replaced the original theme of the folk legend by the more dramatic one of the horror of old age and the decay of love, and Deirdre says to Naisi: 'Isn't it a small thing is foretold about the ruin of ourselves, Naisi, when all men have age coming and great ruin in the end.'

It is clear that Synge was thinking of his own death when he wrote such lines as 'Death should be a poor, untidy thing, though it's a queen that dies.' His obsessions in this play with 'the filth of the grave' spurred him to emphasize the vitality, the wilfulness and wild beauty of the heroine which appears in the farewell scene, where Deirdre says: 'Go to your brothers. For seven years you have been kindly, but the hardness of death has come beween us.' There was a deep poignancy in the acting of Molly Allgood that night which I have never felt in any subsequent performance I have seen of the play; a ghostly quality, as though the slight brown-eyed girl with her pale face, the embodiment of tragedy, still lingered under the hypnotic spell of the dead author, moving about the stage as in a trance, and her voice had the ring of uncontrollable pathos when she murmured: 'I have put away sorrow like a shoe that is worn out and muddy, for it is I have had a life that will be envied by great companies. It was not by a low birth I made kings uneasy, and they sitting in the halls of Emain.'

Every play Synge wrote was part of a general attack on the drama of his day and this is clearly demonstrated in the three short but significant prefaces to *The Playboy of the Western World*, *The Tinker's Wedding* and *Poems and Translations* in which he defended his plays and enunciated his theories of creative literature. Synge's protest, a double one, was directed on the one hand against Yeats who held that only poetic plays were serious plays, and on the other against Edward Martyn[7] and George Moore,[8] who were in favour of a drama which depicted the ordinary life of men and women divorced from poetry. Synge saw that those three men were leading the

newly-created Abbey Theatre in a false direction. Yeats had prophesied that the Irish theatre of the future would discover its material in national legend and the immense store house of Celtic mythology and folklore, and wrote: 'Our plays will be for the most part remote, spiritual and ideal.' George Moore and Edward Martyn, on the other hand, following the example of Ibsen, hoped that the playwrights of the future would write psychological and social plays dealing with Irish life. Moore had already given the public an example of the former in *The Strike of Arlingford*[9] and Edward Martyn one of the latter in *The Heather Field*,[10] an Ibsenite play in an Irish setting. Synge in his plays and prefaces was hitting at those two kinds of drama, the poetic drama and the social drama: in *The Playboy* he presents a contrast to Edward Martyn's vision of the Irish countryside in *The Heather Field*, while his *Deirdre of the Sorrows* is intended as a counterblast to AE's and Yeats's *Deirdre*,[11] both of which he considered too remote and unreal. AE's *Deirdre* is a dreamy, pantheistic, undramatic evocation of the ancient legend; the characters are distant diaphanous phantoms, flitting through the shining mountains in the purple misty dawns of 'the many-coloured land'. Synge's *Deirdre* was written in strong reaction against such mysticism, as was also the following short poem entitled 'The Passing of the Shee', written after he had seen one of AE's fairy pictures:

> Adieu, sweet Angus, Maeve and Fand,
> Ye plumed yet skinny Shee,
> That poets played with hand in hand
> To learn their ecstasy.
> We'll stretch in Red Dan Sally's ditch,
> And drink in Tubber fair,
> Or poach with Red Dan Philly's bitch
> The badger and the hare.

Yeats in later years believed there was greater similarity between Synge's theories and his own and Lady Gregory's than ever was the case.

Synge's death marked the end of a chapter in the history of the Irish National Theatre. Throughout his last year he was anguished by the realization that while his physical strength was declining his mental perceptions were growing more acute. My friend Jack Larchet gave me a moving description of the death of Synge. He kept working away feverishly at *Deirdre of the Sorrows* and had reached the third act.[12] Years before Molly Allgood had had strange premonitions of his death: one day when she and Synge were sitting in a tea-shop, as she was looking at him, the flesh suddenly seemed to fall from his face and all she could see was a skull, and just before his operation in 1908, when she was full of hopes that he would be cured, she dreamed that she saw him in a coffin being lowered into the grave. 'In the early morning of March 24, 1909,' Jack Larchet said to me, 'he said to the nurse, "it is no use fighting death any longer", and he turned over and died.'

NOTES

For a note on Walter Starkie see p. 47.

1. Finn MacCoul (Fionn MacCumhal). Variants Finn, Find. Same as Fingal, identified in the Fenian cycle of legends as the Fianna's champion of Ireland, superhuman in size, strength, speed and prowess.
2. For a note on Cuchulain see p. 94.
3. Queen of Connaught, wife of King Ailill. She coveted the Brown Bull of Ulster which caused the famous war celebrated in the Gaelic saga, yet after capturing it her White Bull and the Brown Bull fought each other to death. Bulls were deemed huge rebirths of semidivinities.
4. John F. Larchet, R.I.A.M., Conductor of the Abbey Theatre Orchestra.
5. Devoted wife of Cuchulain.
6. The King of Ulster, reputed to have expired in rage over the crucifixion of Christ. He formed the 'Red Branch' military order with his relatives.
7. For a note on Edward Martyn see p. 105.
8. For a note on George Moore see p. 104.
9. *The Strike of Arlingford* (1893).
10. *The Heather Field* had its first production by the Irish Literary Theatre on 9 May 1899.
11. *Deirdre*, by AE, was first produced at the Abbey Theatre on 2 April 1902. Yeats's *Deirdre* had its première on 24 November 1906. Synge's *Deirdre of the Sorrows* was first presented on 13 January 1910. For a full comparison of the three plays see Francis Bickley, 'Deirdre', *Irish Review* (Dublin) (July 1912) p. 252.
12. The most unhappy aspect of Synge's love to Molly Allgood was his constant complaining about his ordinary griefs and his not so ordinary fears about his health. He was haunted by the fact that compared to her he was old. In *Deirdre of the Sorrows*, the play about a young girl betrothed to an old man and in love with a young one, Synge was writing from the depths of his own consciousness as he had never written before. The sense of tragedy which motivates every line in that play, unrelieved by any humour, is not due to the thought of his own impending death as much as to forebodings about his marriage.

Index

Page numbers followed by the letter n indicate that the reference is to a note.

Abbey Theatre, 29n, 30, 71n, 99
  disturbances during first performances of *The Playboy*, 38–47, 49, 50, 55, 61, 68, 100, 101, 125–7, 131
  management, 90, 102
  plans to build, 97
  Yeat's plans to enlarge, 57
AE *see* Russell, George
Allgood, Molly [Maire O'Neill], 2n, 70–6, 124, 125, 132
  in *Deirdre of the Sorrows*, 132
  in *The Playboy*, 51, 72, 73
  premonitions of Synge's death, 133
Allgood, Sarah, 26, 72
Aran Islands
  and plot of *The Playboy*, 117
  and plot of *Shadow of the Glen*, 27
  visited by Joyce, 21n
  visited by Lady Gregory, 86
  visited by Synge, 16, 18, 23, 26, 27, 58, 86, 117, 118
  visited by Yeats, 15
The Aran Islands, 59, 60, 95
  difficulty in publishing, 89
Armonde Dramatic Society, 29n

Bailey, Sir W. H., 104n
Ball, Sir Charles, 70, 92
Ballaghadereen Company, 92
Bennett, Arnold, 30
Best, Dr Richard, 9n, 47n, 96, 103, 114–20, 127
Boucicault, Dion, 29n
Bourgeois, Maurice, 13
Boyle, William, 51
Bullen, A. H., 89

Carelton, William, 27
Castle Kevin, 3, 4
Clinch, Kitty, 70
Colum, Pádraic, 69n
Corot, Jean-Baptiste-Camille, 3, 4
The Countess Cathleen, 94n
Crane, Stephen, 117
Cuchulain of Muirthemme, 87

Dana, 1, 6, 96
Davis, Thomas Osborne, 61n
Davitt, Michael, 107
Defoe, Daniel, 67
Deirdre [Russell], 133
Deirdre [Yeats], 65, 86, 133
Deirdre of the Sorrows, 2n, 61, 68, 93, 103, 127, 132, 133
Digges, Dudley, 24
Dirane, Pat, 27
Dublin Evening Mail, 51

Eglinton, John [William K. Magee], 96
Elmassian, Michel, 8
Empedocles on Etna, 61
Etude Morbide, 2n
Evans, Caradoc, 27

Family Herald, 30
Fay, Frank J., 29n
Fay, William G., 24, 29n, 38, 91, 102
  in *The Playboy*, 68, 124
Fortnightly, 89

Gaelic League, 14, 65, 92
Glen Cullen, 2n
Gogarty, Oliver St. John, 35, 102, 118, 121, 123

INDEX

Goldsmith, Oliver, 111
Gonne, Maude, 5, 7n, 13
Great Queen Street Theatre, 86n
Gregory, Lady, 5, 7n, 22, 45n, 77, 86–93, 121, 124
    support for *The Playboy*, 42
    use of dialect, 87
Griffith, Arthur, 28, 51
Gwynn, Stephen, 29n

Hardy, Thomas, 48
Haynes, Mary, 72
Hearn, Lafcadio, 67
The Heather Field, 94n, 133
Hemans, Felicia, 64
Herrick, Robert, 128
Horniman, Annie, 26, 30, 71n, 97
Houghton, C. H. *see* Matheson, Cherrie
Hyacinth Halvey, 77, 88
Hyde, Dr Douglas, 37n, 45n, 87

Ibsen, H., 21
Iceland Fisherman, 66
In the Shadow of the Glen, 19, 22–8, 55, 59, 61, 63, 64, 82, 88, 89, 120, 122
    first production, 64, 120
    suggestion of the plot, 27
In West Kerry, 62n
Inishmaan *see* Aran Islands
Irish Homestead, 47n
Irish National Dramatic Company, 25n
Irish National Theatre Society, 25n, 64

Johnson, Brinsley, 89
Joyce, James, 20, 21, 66, 123

Kickham, Charles Joseph, 62n
The King's Threshold, 26, 64
Kingsway Theatre, 83

Lady Windemere's Fan, 30
Larchet, Jack, 131, 133
Longworth, Francis, 105n
Loti, Pierre, 66, 81, 117
Lynch, Arthur, 7–13
Lynchehaun, James, 37n

MacBride, John, 63

MacKenna, Stephen, 7–9, 12, 13, 63, 114–16
McKenna, Stephen, 12
Magee, W. K. *see* Eglinton, John
Mair, John, 72
Mair, Pegeen, 72
Marot, Clement, 103
Martyn, Edward, 99–101, 132, 133
Masefield, John, 118
Matheson, Cherrie, 2n, 3–6, 113
Mathews, Elkin, 89
Le Médecin malgré lui, 90
Mitchell, Susan, 51
Molesworth Hall, 25n, 64, 120
Monthly Review, 89
Moore, George, 77, 88, 104n, 132, 133

Nutt, Alfred, 89

O'Donoghue, David James, 20n
O'Donovan, Fred, 124
O Faolain, Sean, 12
O'Keefe, John, 29n
O'Leary, John, 14n, 15, 17
O'Neill, Eugene, 53
O'Neill, Maire *see* Allgood, Molly
Origin of Species, 112
O'Sullivan, Seamus, 111, 116, 123, 128

The Passing of the Shee, 133
Patrick Street, 1, 4
Pearse, Padraic, 69n
The Playboy of the Western World, 13, 19, 35, 36, 48–53, 59, 67, 68, 71–3, 90, 91, 123, 125
    allusion to Arthur Lynch, 10, 12
    cuts in script, 91
    disturbance during first performances *see* Abbey Theatre
    first London performance, 83, 84
    suggestion of the plot, 117
Plymouth Brethren, 113
Poems and Translations, 132
Power, Arthur, 21n
Prelude, 2n
Purser, Sarah, 104n
Pygmalion, 49

Quinn, John, 90

Quinn, Maire, 24

Racine, Jean-Baptiste, 103
Radio Eireann, 73
Richards, Grant, 89
Riders to the Sea, 19, 43, 59, 61, 63, 66, 82, 88, 89, 121
   attention to detail in production, 121
Roberts, George, 119–28
Rogers, William Robert, 129n
Ross, Florence, 6n
Russell, George [AE], 25n, 47n, 66, 99, 133
Ryan, F. M., 2n, 90

Samhain, 89
Scott, C. P., 61n
Shadow of the Glen see In the Shadow of the Glen
Shaw, G. B., 49, 118, 127
The Speaker, 8, 14, 18
Starkey, James Sullivan *see* O'Sullivan, Seamus
Starkie, Walter F., 47n
Stephens, Edward, 6n, 112–14, 117, 119, 122, 128
The Strike of Arlingford, 133
Symons, Arthur, 94n
Synge, Alec, 117
Synge, John Millington
   and art, 116
   articles on the 'Congested Districts' of the west of Ireland, 61n
   at Castle Kevin, 3, 4
   at first London performance of *The Playboy*, 83, 84
   at rehearsals, 23, 35, 123, 124
   death of, 70, 71, 74–7, 94, 103, 104, 111, 128, 133
   reported in Irish press, 76
   described by
      A. Lynch, 10, 12
      Cherrie Matheson, 3
      E. Stephens, 119
      G. Moore, 102
      J. Masefield, 78, 79
      J. B. Yeats, 106
      Maire Nic Shiubhlaigh, 23
      P. Colum, 62
      W. Starkie, 131
   dialect in plays, 26, 27, 53, 99, 121
   difficulty in finding publisher, 88, 89
   director of Irish National Theatre Society, 90
   and Gaelic League, 14, 65, 92
   German review of work, 87
   and Hodgkins Disease, 7n
   and honesty, 113
   in Aran Islands, 16, 18, 23, 26, 27, 58, 86, 117, 118
   in Black Forest, 58
   in Bloomsbury, 80
   in Kingstown, 4, 64, 68, 111, 131
   in Paris, 1, 4, 5, 8–11, 15–18, 95–7, 106, 108, 114, 115
   influence of MacKenna, 8, 12, 14
   influence of Wordsworth, 1, 2n, 3
   interviewed after disturbances during performance of *The Playboy*, 38–42, 44
   love of countryside, 108–10
   member of Dublin Naturalists' Field Club, 129n
   mother, 112, 114
   and occultism, 109
   origin of surname, 113
   poems, 57, 58, 84, 85
   and politics, 13, 14, 56, 80, 87
   portrait by J. B. Yeats, 107n, 125
   prefaces, 132
   and reading, 65
   relatives attitude toward, 70, 71
   and religion, 4, 80, 112
   at time of death, 70, 71, 128
   and spelling, 6n
   and telepathy, 5
   throat operation, 5, 7n
   views on tourism in Ireland, 83
   and the violin, 4, 18, 82, 96
   walking stick, 62, 63
   with tinkers, 98
   and writing, 107, 108, 123
Synge, Mary, 129n

The Tinker's Wedding, 21, 61, 132
Tobin, Paddy, 45
Traits and Stories of the Irish Peasant, 27
Tullira Castle, 105n

Ulysses, 21n, 37n, 47n
Under Ether, 7n
United Irishman, 28
Unwin, Fisher, 89

Villon, François, 103
Vita Vecchia, 6n

The Well of the Saints, 30, 31, 48, 59, 92, 93, 99
  suggestion of the plot, 67
When the Moon Has Set, 2n, 94n
Whitbread, J. W., 29n
Wilde, Oscar, 115
Wogan Brown girls, 45

Wordsworth, W., 1, 2n, 3
The Workhouse Ward, 92
Wright, Adolphus, 124

Yeats, Jack B., 34n, 61n, 103, 125
Yeats, John B., 63
Yeats, W. B., 1, 5, 13, 15–17, 26, 36, 61n, 85n, 86–8, 91, 95–8, 103, 132
  and management of Abbey Theatre, 102
  on future of Irish theatre, 133
Young Ireland Society of Paris, 9n, 16

Zola, Emile, 49